Ancient India's Imprints and I

ANCIENT INDIA'S IMPRINTS AND INFLUENCES ON THE WORLD

With Best Wishes

Sanjana

NITIN MEHTA

28/7/2024

The Mandir

Coulsdon

Divine Destination

Subsidiary Alliance ~ Motilal Banarsidass Publishing House

Divine Destination

naraina@mlbd.in

www.mlbd.in

First Edition : Delhi, 2023

ISBN: 978-93-91024-94-9 (Hardcover)
ISBN: 978-93-91024-47-5 (Paperback)

Printed & Published by
Rajendra P Jain *for*
Motilal Banarsidass Publishing House
A-44, Naraina Industrial Area, Phase I,
New Delhi–110 028 (INDIA)
Email: naraina@mlbd.in
Website: www.mlbd.in

Foreword

Throughout history, many nations and civilisations have been born, some of which have flourished and established their presence across large parts of the world. Inevitably, however, with the passing of time, they flounder and a new force emerges in a different part of the world, which reaches even more parts of the globe and establishes its hegemony. In some cases, the domination over other nations and races lasts for hundreds of years. Nonetheless, there is nothing permanent in this impermanent world. This is a core belief of Eastern religions. Unstoppable time ushers in new situations and circumstances that lead to the decay of the old and the creation of the new. Civilisations have appeared and disappeared without a trace. The Aztec, Roman, Greek, Mughal, British and many other empires have become a footnote in history.

The Indian civilisation – which is the oldest living civilisation, going back tens of thousands of years – has reached its zenith too, and it has impacted almost all the continents of the world. There is one crucial difference between the Indian empire and the other powerful empires throughout history: the latter conquered with the might of the sword, but India conquered through its ancient heritage, which had an immensely rich culture, an advanced knowledge of science and mathematics, and a mature, well-established political system. Non-violence and respect for indigenous cultures are the hallmarks of how India established its influence over many different races and cultures throughout the world. For many, India was the cradle of human civilisation.

India's downfall started with the invasion from Arabia in the 12th century, and continued through the rule of the Mughals – the Muslim dynasty of Turkic-Mongol origin who ruled most of northern India from the early 16th to the mid-18th century. Next came the Persian invasion under Nader Shah, who defeated the Mughals, and, ultimately, the invasion and rule of the British from the 18th century onwards for around 200 years. Crucially, though, unlike other civilisations, the Indian civilisation did not perish. The reason for its survival lies in the depth and strength of India's heritage.

This book takes the reader on a journey through ancient India's influences and imprints on the rest of the world. There have been many thinkers, philosophers, archaeologists, geographers and historians in the West who have spared no words in their praise of what India represented. However, these voices were drowned out as the mighty British Empire conquered a huge swathe of the globe.

One thing I have learnt from writing this book is that the things people do in the name of their country or religion or race and the extent to which people are motivated to kill hundreds of thousands of people in the name of an ideology is so unfortunate, not least because their own future generations will turn against what was so sacred to them. Almost 500 years ago, Ireland was a non-Christian country with its own set of beliefs and traditions. The advent of Christianity, its split between Protestants and Catholics, and the violence that has taken place between the factions would not be comprehensible to the pre-Christian generations. Similarly, tens of thousands of British youth turned against colonialism and slavery, which was something that was so important to their forefathers. With the arrival of the ideology of communism, tens of thousands of youth became iconoclasts, smashing statues of Buddha in China, who was such a revered figure for the forefathers of these youths. From the 1950s onwards, the ideological divide between capitalism and communism was so great that a nuclear war was a distinct possibility. For today's youth, this seems to be the most frivolous thing that could have been done, which would have killed tens of thousands of people in the name of an ideology. In an impermanent world, your own will turn against you!

The only solution is non-violence, which should justify the means to an end. This is not pacifism. Violence could be justified to defend the nation or your heritage, but only as a last resort.

Nitin Mehta

Table of Contents

The ancient Hindus of yore were not simply spiritual people, always busy with mystical problems and never troubling themselves with the questions of 'this world'... India also has its Napoleons and Charlemagnes, its Bismarcks and Machiavellis. But the real charm of Indian history does not consist in these aspirants after universal power, but in its peaceful and benevolent Imperialism—a unique thing in the history of mankind. The colonisers of India did not go with swords and fire in their hands; they used... the weapons of their superior culture and religion... The Buddhist age has attracted special attention, and the French savants have taken much pains to investigate the splendid monuments of the Indian cultural empire in the Far East.

– Sylvian Levi (1863–1935),
French orientalist and Indologist
(Bayley, 2004)

Shiva Linga, known as the Lia Fáil, in Ireland (JohnJDuncan, 2012). CC BY-SA 4.0.

According to Vaishnava Das (2015): *In County Meath, Ireland, on the Hill of Tara sits a mysterious stone known as the Lia Fáil (Stone of Destiny). According to* The Annals of the Four Masters, *an ancient document written by Franciscan Monks between 1632-1636 AD, this stone was brought to Ireland by the Tuatha Dé Danann, a supernaturally gifted people. Some speculate it was they who brought the power to make bronze to Ireland. They were the main deities of pre-Christian Gaelic Ireland.*

The Great Celtic–India Connection

'Bengal to Donegal!' (Serkeen, 2017)

Peter Berresford Ellis – British historian, literary biographer and novelist – explained in detail the Druid-India connection (cited in Merlin, 2020). Ireland was one of the few countries in Europe and North Africa that had still not been conquered by Rome by the fifth century. It had a vibrant culture, and its people believed in many gods. The Celtic culture and Gaelic language of the people of Ireland have striking similarities with the Indian civilisation and the Sanskrit language. The Old Gaelic word '*aire*' (Irish) means noble, which is the same as the Sanskrit word '*arya*'. The Celtic name for the River Thames is the Tamesis, which means dark river. A tributary of the Ganges is called the Tamas. '*Tamas*' in Sanskrit also means dark or negative. The River Thames is therefore a name of Sanskrit origin! The word for 'soul' is '*anam*' in Gaelic and it is '*atma*' in Sanskrit. The king in Gaelic is called the '*Rig*', which along with the English word 'reign' and the German word '*Reich*' are all from the Sanskrit-origin word '*Raja*' meaning king. Ancient bardic poetry and poems of praise in Celtic Ireland were in a similar tradition to the Hindu Vedic system. Celtic cosmology is parallel to the Vedic Hindu cosmology, which is based on 27 lunar houses called '*nakshatras*'. Celtic gods are called '*deuos*' and the Hindu gods are called '*devas*'. For generations, the Celtic people had passed on the story of the goddess Danu. '*Danu*' means divine waters. A story of the goddess Danu also appears in Vedic scriptures, and it has the same meaning. The famous River Danube, which runs through many European countries, derives its name from the goddess Danu. The Celtic god Lugh is very similar to the Vedic god Indra. Both carry thunderbolts. The Celts believed in the transmigration of the soul, just as Hindus do. The Druids were an integral part of Celtic society. They were held in high esteem. Druids respected nature and animals. They were like the Brahmins of India. Their occupations included being seers, healers, royal advisors and judges. The Celts had four divisions of society, just like the Indian system of four classes: *Brahmin* (intellectuals), *Kshatriya* (warriors and rulers), *Vaishya* (mercantile and farmers) and *Shudra* (artisans).

Song of Amairgen and the *Bhagavad Gita*

Amairgen was the first Druid to arrive in Ireland. According to Berresford Ellis (cited in Merlin, 2020), 'In this song Amairgen subsumes everything into his own being with a philosophic outlook that parallels the declaration of Krishna in the *Bhagavad Gita*.'

The Song of Amairgen (cited in Merlin, 2020)

I am the wind that blows across the sea;
I am the wave of the ocean;
I am the murmur of the billows;
I am the ox of the seven combats;
I am the vulture on the rock;
I am a beam of the sun;
I am the fairest of flowers;
I am a wild boar in valour;
I am a salmon in the pool;
I am a lake on the plain;
I am the skill of the craftsman;
I am a word of science;
I am the spear point that gives battle;
I am the God who creates in the head of man the fire of thought.

Who is it that enlightens the assembly upon the mountain, if not I?
Who tells the ages of the moon, if not I?
Who shows the place where the sun goes to rest, if not I?
Who is the God that fashions enchantments – The enchantment of battle and the wind of change?

In comparison, Lord Krishna in the *Bhagavad Gita*, Chapter 10 says this:

I am the electric Force in the powers of nature
I am the mind
and I am the intelligence in all that lives,
I am the Whirlwind among the winds
of the waters, I am the Ocean
I am the Thunderbolt of weapons
of cows I am the Cow of Plenty
I am the Eagle among birds
I am the passion in those who procreate
I am the eternal present,
I am the lion among beasts
I am the beginning, the middle and the end in creation
I am time inexhaustible
I am all devouring death
I am the origin of all that shall happen
Whatever is glorious, excellent, beautiful and mighty,
be assured that it comes from but a fragment of my splendour.

The greatest poet-philosopher of Ireland, William Butler Yeats (1865–1939), was deeply influenced by Hindu thought. A few years before his death, he said: 'I have fed on the philosophy of the *Upanishads* all my life.' His Indophilia began when he attended a talk by Mohini Chatterjee, a theosophist and Vedantist, in Dublin in December 1885. At the young age of 24, he wrote three poems featuring India: 'The Indian to His Love', 'Anushaya and Vijaya' and 'The Indian Upon God'.

On 7th July 1912, Yeats met India's great poet Rabindranath Tagore. Yeats wrote an introduction for *Gitanjali*, a collection of poems written by Tagore. According to the The Open University (n.d.), Yeats also met Shri Purohit Swami, who was a poet, philosopher and Hindu monk. Similarly, Yeats wrote an introduction to Swami's autobiography: *The Autobiography of an Indian Monk: His Life and Adventures*. Among other things, Shri Swami and Yeats worked together to translate *The 10 Principal Upanishads*. This was done in Majorca during the years 1935 and 1936.

In Europe from the 1790s onwards, there was a surge of interest in Indian culture and metaphysics. *Shakuntala*, the great folklore play written by the fifth-century poet and playwright Kalidasa, heralded this new respect and understanding of India. It was first translated into English by Sir William Jones in 1789. Over the years, 46 other translations in 12 European languages were completed. It is a sweet irony that Ashok Varadkar, the father of the former Taoiseach (leader) of Ireland Leo Varadkar, is from Mumbai.

The onset of Christianity from the fifth century onwards resulted in the almost complete disappearance of the Celtic and Druid faiths and cultures from Ireland.

Ancient India and its people, who were known as Aryans, had spread its influence throughout many parts of the world.

Heliodorus Pillar, Vidishā, Madhya Pradesh, India
(Dilipkumarftii1977, 2020).

The Great Greece–India Connection

On a holiday to the Greek island of Crete a few years ago, we took a day trip to visit archaeological sites. At one spot, the tour guide said that people in the area used to worship the goddess Gayatri. I asked my wife if she had heard of the word 'Gayatri', and she said yes. I spoke to the tour guide and told him that we still worship the goddess Gayatri. He said he was not surprised and there was a Hindu influence. The Greeks were impressed with the Vedic culture as far back as 200 BCE. We can see this evidence in what is called the Heliodorus column, which was erected by the Greek ambassador to India in 113 BCE at Besnagar in central India (located in the present-day city of Vidisha in Madhya Pradesh).The inscription on the column, as published in the *Journal of the Royal Asiatic Society* (1909, cited in Hebner and Rosen, n.d.), says this:

> *This Garuda column of Vasudeva (Vishnu), the god of gods, was erected here by Heliodorus, a worshipper of Vishnu, the son of Dion, and an inhabitant of Taxila, who came as Greek ambassador from the Great King Antialkidas to King Kasih Putra Bhagya Bhadra, the Savior, then reigning prosperously in the fourteenth year of his kingship. Three important precepts when practiced lead to heaven: self-restraint, charity, conscientiousness.*

This shows that Heliodorus had become a worshipper of Vishnu and was well versed in the Hindu texts.

There are statues of Greek men wearing an Indian *dhoti* with a Vaishnava mark on their forehead. The Greeks were known as 'Yavanas' in India, and there is a mention of them in the *Mahabharata*.

The legendary story of Hercules has parallels to stories of Krishna and Balaram. Hercules killed many demons as a child, and one of the stories was of him killing a demon who came to breastfeed him. It is an exact replica of the story of Krishna killing Putana. So many other adventures of Krishna are similar to the adventures of Hercules.

Plato's (428–347 BCE) book *Phaedrus* follows similar themes to the *Bhagavad Gita*. The idea of the soul, its release from the body, and its transmigration are all explored by Plato. The chariot allegory mentioned in the *Katha Upanishad* (1:3:3–9), one of the oldest and most important *Upanishads*, is also used by Plato. The following is a brief translation of the allegory by Charles Johnston (Universal Theosophy, 2020):

> *Know the Higher Self as the lord of the chariot, and the body as the chariot; know the soul as the charioteer, and the mind and emotional nature as the reins. They say that the powers of perception and action are the horses, and that objective things are the roadways for these; the Self joined with the powers through the mental and emotional nature is called the enjoyer of experience by the wise.*

In the *Mahabharata*, the allegory is brought to life in the characters of Krishna (the lord of the chariot); Arjuna, who rides as the passenger, but also directs Krishna where to go with the chariot; the horses; and, lastly, the entire setting – for Arjuna directs Krishna to move the chariot between the two opposing armies, which themselves symbolise the lower and the higher nature. The whole of the *Bhagavad Gita* can be read as a kind of unfoldment of the allegory first given in the *Katha Upanishad*.

Aristotle's (382–322 BCE) *De Anima* has parallels with the *Upanishads*. Bradley Y. Bartholomew (2017), an independent researcher, presents in his paper an original interpretation of the

Upanishads in that the inner self is located in the embryo-brain region of the brain. It is the part of the brain that operates during dreaming and deep sleep, and it causes the transition from the sleeping to the waking state, and the *Upanishads* state unequivocally that the self is responsible for these mental states. Aristotle arrives at the same conclusion.

All the great Greek philosophers were fervent vegetarians. Plutarch, Aristotle, Plato, Pythagoras and Socrates were all vegetarians and promoted a vegetarian lifestyle. They also believed in the fundamental Hindu ideas of the eternal soul, reincarnation and the idea that the external world that we perceive through the senses is ultimately unreal. Plato, in his book *Republic* (circa 375 BCE) recommends that an ideal city should be a vegetarian city. He also said that an ideal society should be divided into four groups, just as in the Hindu system.

Greek poet Homer was the author of *The Iliad* and *The Odyssey* (believed to have been composed between the eighth and seventh centuries BCE); these epic poems were passed down orally by bards long before they were written down. *The Iliad* has almost the same story as the *Mahabharata*. Just as in the *Mahabharata*, *The Iliad* has two warring camps, which resulted in a 14-day war. Pallavi Mishra (2020) describes the similarities between the two epics in detail. Here is one of her observations:

> *The Trojan war starts with the reluctance of Achilles, just like Arjuna before the Mahabharata war asks Krishna to take him to the centre of the field, and after seeing both the armies' formation, he refuses to fight.*
>
> *Another striking similarity is that in the Mahabharata war scene, Sanjaya describes the war scene by scene to the blind king Dhritrastra, using his extraordinary vision; while in the Iliad, during the Trojan war, the Trojan king was watching all the events sitting in the fort wall, with his minister narrating to him all the events of the war.*

The Odyssey bears huge likenesses to the *Ramayana*. Both Lord Rama and Odysseus were eager to be reunited with their wives from whom they had been separated; Sita in the case of Lord Rama, and Penelope in the case of Odysseus. Both women were dedicated to their husbands. Sita rejected Ravana's offers of marriage, as did Penelope spurn the offers of many who wanted to marry her.

Alexander the Great invaded India in 362 BCE. He was confronted by the Hindu king Porus. Fatigued by wars, Alexander's men revolted and refused to go further into India. Alexander had to return. While in India, Alexander came into contact with Hindu ascetics and in a conversation with them, he was told this:

> *King Alexander, every man can possess only so much of the earth's surface as this we are standing on. You are but human like the rest of us, save that you are always busy and up to no good, travelling so many miles from your home, a nuisance to yourself and to others. Ah well! You will soon be dead, and then you will own just as much of this earth as will suffice to bury you.*

Alexander was impressed by the ascetics and took one of them, who was called Calanus, with him.

After the death of Alexander, the mighty empire of Chandragupt Mauyra defeated the Greek forces. He married a Greek princess, Helena, and a peace treaty was signed between the two powers.

One of the later and lengthier accounts of Western interactions with Indian ascetic wise men occurs in a third-century biography of the ascetic wise man Apollonius of Tyana. Written by a sophist named Philostratus, *The Life of Apollonius of Tyana* describes in great length and detail Apollonius's journey to India and his conversations with the Indian sages, known as the 'Wise Ones'.

Sir William Temple (1628–1699) declared that 'Indian philosophers were the originators of the Greek ideas of vegetarianism to eternity of matter' (1685, cited in Stuart, 2008).

John Archibald Wheeler (1911–2008) – an eminent American physicist, who was the first one to be involved in the theoretical development of the atomic bomb – suggested: 'I would like to think that someone will trace how the deepest thinking of India made its way to Greece and from there to the philosophy of our times.'

Buddhism and the Greeks

Under the patronage of Emperor Ashoka (268–232 BCE), Buddhism spread all over Asia.

Greek monks played a direct role in the upper hierarchy of Buddhism and in its early dissemination. During the reign (165–135 BCE) of the Greco-Bactrian ruler King Menader I, the Mahadharmaraksita (literally translated to mean 'Great Teacher' or 'Preserver of the *Dharma*') was Greek. Bactria was in Central Asia – in what is present-day Turkmenistan, Afghanistan, Uzbekistan and Tajikistan – and was populated by Persian Zoroastrians and Buddhists.

At the time of Alexander the Great, the Greeks conquered a large part of Asia, from Asia Minor to modern day Afghanistan, Pakistan and the north-east of India. The Greek influence continued after Alexander's death, as a number of Greek kingdoms were founded in Asia. Evidence of the Buddhist expansion during the Indo-Greek period (starting in 180 BCE) comes from coins, the significant number of *stupas*[1] built during that period, and statues depicting Buddha accompanied by Greek gods and goddesses. In Greco-Buddhist culture and art, Greek gods are considered to be guardians of Buddha or are represented as angels accompanying Buddha during important events in his life. The statues of Buddha are actually protected by Hellenic gods.

According to Neos Alexandria (n.d.):

> *The religion that is practiced by the Indo-Greeks who followed Buddhist philosophy but who continued to adhere to the Greek* nomos arkhaios *(customs and cultures) is known as Greco-Buddhism* [...]

1 A *thupa* or *stupa* is a hemispherical structure containing relics and is used as a place of meditation.

> *Greco-Buddhism or Hellenic Buddhism can be seen in two ways. It can be seen as the cultural and religious syncretism between the Hellenic culture and Buddhism. Alternatively it can be seen as the adoption of the Buddhist philosophy by a person with a Hellenic background* [...]
>
> *Buddhism* [...] *and spread quite rapidly among the Greeks of Alexandria of the Caucasus and Taxila to the point that in Asoka's time these were main Buddhist centres. In the* Mahavamsa *one of the high monks present in the devotion of the high* Thupa *was a Yona (Greek) monk called Dharmarikkita who brought 30,000 Greek monks from Alexandria to the Caucasus to join him. A monk with the same name was sent North by Asoka to spread the Rock Edicts*[2] *in the Greco-Bactrian lands. On an interesting note early Buddhist[s] in Sri Lanka base[d] upon the* Mahavamsa *went to Alexandria of the Caucasus to learn Buddhism.*

The arrival of the Roman Empire, along with Christianity, spelled the end of Greek heritage. There was wholesale destruction of the statues of what were considered to be pagan gods. Christians came to be known as 'those who move that which should not be moved'. The Celtic culture of Ireland disappeared after the arrival of Christianity; the Mayan, Olmec and Aztec civilisations were destroyed by Spanish Christian conquistadors; and the Greek Hellenic traditions disappeared with the arrival of Christianity. By contrast, Buddhism spread all over Asia in harmony with local cultures and traditions. There was no destruction of local icons or traditions.

2 The rock edicts of Ashoka are inscriptions engraved on large stones and cave walls; they exhort people to live peacefully and follow good moral conduct.

The Great Macedonia–India Connection

(The Republic of North Macedonia was part of the former Yugoslavia up to 1991.)

Indian Sanskritist Durga Prasad Shastri made the following observation:

> *When I was in Moscow staying at a resort, they gave me the key to my room 234, and told me:* 'dwesta tridesyat chetiri'... *In disbelief I stood there incredulous to my own ears – Was I in front of a young lady in Moscow, or in Benares or Ujjain some 2,500 years ago?*

This same number in Sanskrit is pronounced '*dwishata tridasha chatwari*'. How could this self-evident uniformity be possible? How could these two languages have preserved their common ancient pronunciation to such a degree until today?

There is little doubt that the Aryans from India settled in what is Macedonia today.

According to Chulev (2016), 60 per cent of word roots in the Macedonian language are common to Sanskrit. The very structures of the idioms are identical to Sanskrit. The two languages share the same grammatical base. Both are written with syllables and consonant-vowel symbols.

Here is a short list of words listed by Chulev (2016) that are similar in Sanskrit and Macedonian:

Macedonian	Sanskrit	English
Odavya	*Advaya*	Free from duplicity
Alayaz	*Alasya*	Lazy
Mande	*Anda*	Egg
Kantar	*Antar*	In the middle
Zapovedi	*Apvada*	Orders, command
As	*Ashva*	Stallion, horse
Osthara	*Ashtra*	Sharp spear, weapon
Iskustva	*Astitva*	Existence
Balavasta	*Balavastha*	Child, childish
Baghata	*Baghata*	Rich
Beg(a)	*Bhag*	Escape, run
Bodra	*Bhadra*	Brave, good
Boi	*Bhay*	Afraid
Breman	*Bharman*	Burden, heavy
Basna	*Bhasana*	Speech
Vrne	*Varshana*	Raining
Vastina	*Vastuta*	In reality, the truth
Vedehie	*Vedana*	Vision, knowledge
Vigya	*Vigya*	Sees, knows
Vedova	*Vidahva*	Widow
Vyasaa	*Vyavasaya*	Business, enterprise
Grom-Magla	*Garjanmegha*	Thunder, cloud
Govedo	*Govinda*	Cow-herder
Desna	*Dakshin*	Right
Znam	*Znanam (Gnanam)*	Knowledge
Pozanta	*Znata (Janata)*	Familiar
Kalesha	*Kala*	Dark
Kalender	*Kalena*	Time
Garvan	*Karava*	Crow

Macedonian	Sanskrit	English
Centre	*Kendra*	Centre, place
Tsrna	*Krsna*	Black
Kurovasna	*Kuvasana*	Bad habits
Latitsa	*Lata*	Flower
Med	*Madhu*	Honey
Mandra	*Mandala*	Circle, enclosure
Mrtvosana	*Mritasana*	Dead posture in yoga
Mrtov	*Mrut*	Dead
Mucka	*Mukha*	Mouth
Novstan	*Navasthan*	New place
Novina	*Navin*	News
Padni	*Padi*	To fall
Palava	*Palava*	Foolish, reckless
Piyeshe	*Piyusha*	Drink
Pretvoriti	*Pravrti*	Activist
Predstava	*Prastav*	Suggest
Preanie	*Pradhan*	Teach, transmit
Prekrasna	*Prakasa*	Bright, beautiful
Radost	*Rada, Radhana*	Joy, beautiful
(Baba) Roga	*Roga*	Sickness
Sveda	*Sabda*	Word, love song
Sade	*Sada*	Always
Samaten/Samiten	*Samadhi*	Oneness, alone
Senka	*Sanka*	Doubt
Svekor	*Svar/Svasurah*	Father-in-law
Smee	*Smit*	Smile
Stan	*Sthan*	Dwelling, place
Stup	*Stupa*	Pillar

Macedonian	Sanskrit	English
Srekhya	*Sukha*	Happiness
Tanya	*Tanaya*	Daughter
Triputi	*Triputi*	Triad, three times
Volna	*Urna*	Wool
Haresa	*Harsha*	Joy, happiness
Cigra	*Chakra*	Wheel
Caska	*Casaka*	Glass
Centri	*Chatvari*	Four
So-Ubaa	*Sobha*	Beauty
Yovan	*Yuvaan*	Young (also a name)

While researching this subject, I found out that a film on Macedonia was made by two brothers in 1895. The brothers were born in Greece, but they were of Macedonian origin. Their names will fascinate you. The names are Janaki and Milton, and the surname is Manaki. How could someone of Macedonian origin born in 1878 have the name Janaki? The surname Manaki is also of Sanskrit origin. A *manek* is a semi-precious, brown ruby stone. Lord Swaminarayan (1781–1830) had a famous mare that he rode, which was also called Manaki because of its brown colour!

The lion man from the Stadel cave in Hohlenstein, Lonetal (Bade-Wurtemberg) (Hollmann, 2913). CC BY-SA 4.0.

Lord Narasimha, the man-lion form of the fourth incarnation of Lord Vishnu (Adityamadhav83, 2010). CC BY-SA 3.0.

The Great Germany–India Connection

A nation has been born out of Sanskrit.[3]

The German Empire, also called the Second Reich, was founded on 18th January 1871 in the wake of three short, successful wars by the North German state of Prussia against Austria, Denmark and France. The unification of Germany (excluding Austria and the German-speaking areas of Switzerland) was achieved under the leadership of Chancellor Otto von Bismarck. The new state replaced the German Confederation, a loose association of sovereign states and the highly decentralised Holy Roman Empire.

From the beginning, Germans showed great interest in Sanskrit. The first German scholar of Sanskrit was Heinrich Roth (1620–1668).

Friedrich Von Schlegel (1772–1829) was a poet, philosopher and Indologist. In 1808, he published an epoch-making book, *Über die Sprache und Weisheit der Indier* (meaning *On the Language and Wisdom of India*). Here, he advanced his ideas about religion and, importantly, argued that a people originating from India were the founders of the first European civilisations. Schlegel compared Sanskrit with Latin, Greek, Persian and German, noting many similarities in vocabulary and grammar. He also said 'India is superior in everything, intellectually, religiously or politically and even the Greek heritage seems pale in comparison' (Londhe, 2008).

Friedrich Max Muller (1823–1900) was a German living in Britain. He was the first to translate the *Rig Veda*. He also published *The Sacred Books of the East*, 49 volumes of which appeared between

3 This chapter was originally published as an article in the *Daily Guardian* (Mehta, 2020). It has since been copy-edited before inclusion in this book.

1874 and 1884. His main aim was to convert Hindus to Christianity, and he believed that a thorough study of Hindu scriptures would help him to find the fault lines in what he considered to be a pagan religion. However, he became more and more impressed by what he found in the *Vedas*. This is what he said:

> *If I were asked under what sky the human mind has most fully developed some of its choicest gifts, has most deeply pondered over the greatest problems of life, and has found solutions of some of them which well deserve the attention even of those who have studied Plato and Kant, I should point to India. And if I were to ask myself from what literature we who have been nurtured almost exclusively on the thoughts of Greeks and Romans, and of the Semitic race, the Jewish, may draw the corrective which is most wanted in order to make our inner life more perfect, more comprehensive, more universal, in fact more truly human a life… again I should point to India.*

Johann Gottfried von Herder (1744–1803) was a philosopher and theologist. He said 'Mankind's origins can be traced to India where the human mind got the first shapes of wisdom and virtue.'

In 1791, Kalidasa's play *Shakuntala* made huge waves in Germany. Johann Wolfgang Von Goethe – the German poet, dramatist, biologist, theoretical physicist and polymath – expressed his admiration for *Shakuntala* in the form of a poem. It was translated from German to English by E B Eastwick:

> *If you wish to see the young flowers of Spring and the ready to pluck fruits of Summer at once; or if you wish to see that object which pleases, hypnotises, delights and quenches you at once; or if you wish to see the earth and heaven in one look; I invoke the name of* Shakuntala *and all quests are answered at once.*

So impressed was Goethe with *Shakuntala* that he decided to learn Sanskrit. Goethe also became acquainted with Kalidasa's poem the 'Meghaduta' (meaning 'The Cloud Messenger'). Kalidasa's

'Urvashi Won By Valour' as well as 'Malavika' and 'Agnimitra' were all translated into German between 1827 and 1856. Kalidasa's 'The Birth of the War God' was translated into German prose in 1913.

Johann Goffried von Herder (1744–1803), a philosopher and poet, said this about *Shakuntala*: 'I cannot find a product of the human mind more pleasant than this, a real blossom of the Orient, the first and most beautiful of its kind.' He also said that India is a holy land he yearned for.

Peter von Bohlen (1833) translated *The Three Sataks* by Bhartrahair, the Sanskrit writer and king of Ujjain. *Satakatraya* (in Sanskrit) or *Subhasita Trisati* (in Telugu) is a collection of 300 poems on moral values. The first one, 'Niti Sataka', deals with ethics and morality; the second one, 'Srngara Sataka', deals with man-woman relationships; and the third one, 'Vairagya Sataka' deals with renunciation.

Philologist Franz Bopp (1791–1867) published the book *Analytical Comparison of the Sanskrit, Greek, Latin and Teutonic Languages*, in which he extended to all parts of grammar what he had done in his first book for the verb alone. He had previously published (in 1891) a critical edition, with a Latin translation and notes, of the story of *Nala and Damayanti*, the most beautiful episode of the *Mahabharata*. Other episodes of the *Mahabharata*, such as *Indralokagamanam*, were also published.

Paul Jakob Deussen (1845–1919) was a German Indologist and professor of philosophy at the University of Kiel. He was strongly influenced by Arthur Schopenhauer. He was a friend of Friedrich Nietzsche and Swami Vivekananda. Deussen gave himself the Sanskrit name of Deva-Sena as a mark of his admiration for Hinduism. He is one of the many distinguished Europeans who, often with lyrical admiration, participated in the scholarly Western discovery of Sanskrit and Hinduism that took place in Germany, France and England.

It was when he attended a lecture by Professor Lassen expounding the *Shakuntala* that Deussen was fired up by Sanskrit and Hinduism. His first work was published in English as *The Elements of Metaphysics* in 1894. It was followed by the translations of *The Sutra of the Vedanta* in 1906, *The Philosophy of the Upanishads* in 1908, and *System of the Vedanta* in 1912. After his visit to India in 1904, he wrote a book in English called *My Indian Reminiscences*. It was published in 1912.

August Wilhelm Schlegel was a professor of Sanskrit in Continental Europe and he produced a Latin translation of the *Bhagavad Gita* in 1823. It was the first Sanskrit book printed in Europe. This was the first of a self-financed, self-published series known as *The Indian Library*, which also included translations of the *Ramayana* and the *Hitopadesha*.

In his book *Main Currents in 19th Century Literature* (1872–1890), Danish historian Brandes (1901) wrote this:

> *It was not a surprise that there came a moment in German history when they – the Germans – started to absorb and to utilise the intellectual achievements and the culture of India. It is because this Germany – great, dark and rich in dreams and thoughts – is in reality modern India. Nowhere else in the world history has metaphysics bereft of any empirical research achieved such a high level of development as in ancient India and in modern Germany.*

Wilhelm von Humboldt (1767–1835) was a Prussian philosopher and diplomat. On reading the *Bhagavad Gita*, he said 'I read the poem for the first time today. I felt a sense of overwhelming gratitude to God for having let me be acquainted with this work. It must be the most sublime thing to be found in the world.'

Arthur Schopenhauer (1788–1860), one of the greatest German philosophers and writers stated 'In the whole world there is no study so beneficial and as elevating as that of the *Upanishads*. It has been the solace of my life and will be the solace of my death. They are the product of the highest wisdom. *Vedas* are the most rewarding and the most elevating books possible in the world.'

Werner Heisenberg (1901–1976), Nobel Prize winner and co-founder of quantum physics, articulated that 'after the conversations about Indian philosophy, some of the ideas of quantum physics that had seemed crazy suddenly made much more sense.'

Heinrich Heine (1797–1856) – German romantic, poet, essayist and journalist – explained 'The Portuguese, the Dutch and the English have been for a long time, year after year, shipping home the treasures of India in their big vessels. We Germans have all along been left to watch this. Germany would do likewise but hers would be treasures of spiritual knowledge.'

This explains why Britain did not show the same interest in India's great achievements going back thousands of years. It would be difficult to acknowledge anything positive about the country you have colonised. It would crush any moral justification of enslaving a nation. On the contrary, a narrative would have to be created to show the natives to be uncivilised and backward. Hence, a nation that had brilliant minds and had successfully solved so many unknowns in the field of science, mathematics, astronomy, economics, politics, architecture and a host of other fields was reduced to being called a nation of snake charmers!

Sir Henry Maine, an influential Anglo-Indian scholar and former vice chancellor of Calcutta University, who was also on the Viceroy of India's council, pronounced a view that many Englishmen shared about the unification of Germany: it is a nation born of Sanskrit!

Here are some words that are similar in Sanskrit and German:

German	Sanskrit	English
Kuckuck	*Kokil*	Cuckoo
Wind	*Vaat*	Wind
Bessar	*Behtar*	Better
Witwe	*Vidhva*	Widow
Sitzen	*Sthit*	Sit
Binden	*Bandh*	Bind
Bruder	*Bratha*	Brother
Mutter	*Mata*	Mother
Mischung	*Mishra*	Mix

German	Sanskrit	English
Name	*Naam*	Name
Nasa	*Nasa*	Nose
Mann	*Manu*	Man
Minister	*Mantri*	Minister
Achse	*Aksha*	Axle

Over 40,000-Year-Old Man-Lion Sculpture Found in Germany

Hundreds of thousands of years ago, Lord Narasimha Dev appeared to kill the demon Hiranyakashipu. He had taken the form of half man, half lion. In 1939, an ivory sculpture of a half man, half lion was discovered in Germany. It was found in the Hohlenstein-Stadel, a German cave. It is the oldest piece of art ever found.

The German name for it is *Löwenmensch*, meaning lion-human. It was not until 2009 that all the pieces were put together. A computer simulation produced the half man, half lion image.

Could it be that whoever made this sculpture was a devotee of Lord Narasimha Dev?

By a strange coincidence, the International Society for Krishna Consciousness (ISKCON), a Hare Krishna movement, has a temple and a farming community in the Black Forest area of Germany. It is called Simhachalan. It is the only temple in Europe that has Lord Narasimha as the main deity of worship there. The temple is about 200 kilometres from the site where the lion-human sculpture was found! More than 40,000 years later, Lord Narasimha appears again!

Stranger Than Fiction!

Odin is a prehistoric figure in Germanic legends. He is revered as a godlike figure. He is said to have hung upside down on a tree for seven days and nights, acquiring hidden knowledge of the world from supernatural beings. It was a tree called Yggdrasil, which is a giant ash tree. Odin had only one eye.

In prehistoric Hindu legend, there was a great teacher called Shukracharya. He was the guru and advisor of King Bali. He too hung on a tree to meditate on Lord Shiva to get a boon that would enable him to bring dead people back to life. He too had one eye!

The Unfortunate Connection of Hitler with India

Hitler usurped the Hindu, Jain and Buddhist religious symbol that is known as the swastika in both Sanskrit and German. Hitler's senior commander Heinrich Himmler was known to carry the *Bhagavad Gita* in his pocket. Obviously, he completely misunderstood the core message of the Hindu holy book. Himmler also greatly liked a novel called *Siddhartha*. It was published in 1922. The author was Hermann Hesse, and the story is about the spiritual journey of self-discovery of a man named Siddhartha during the time of the Gautama Buddha.

It is not known if Hitler was vegetarian, but he believed very much in its many benefits. According to Stuart (2008), 'Vegetarianism was an integral part of Hitler's Fascist ideology.' He adds that this does not imply that vegetarianism has anything intrinsically Fascist about it. Stuart (2008) also maintains that Hitler believed that a vegetarian diet could be a key to Germany's military success. Himmler wanted to turn the army into a non-smoking, teetotal, vegetarian force. He believed that Indian vegetarians had longer lives and better health than the Europeans. He even thought that the Aryan German army could take over the world if only they returned to their original vegetarian diet. Rudolf Hess, another senior figure in Hitler's regime, was a strict vegetarian.

Sanskrit in Present-Day Germany

Sanskrit has enjoyed a great revival in Germany. Fourteen universities in Germany teach Sanskrit, as opposed to just four in the UK. Heidelberg University organises Sanskrit-speaking courses in Australia, Europe, North America and even in India! Both Germany and India can be the custodians of Sanskrit!

Vishnu statue excavated in the Volga region of Russia circa seventh to eighth century (Unknown, n.d.)

Burning effigy at Butter Week or Maslenista festival in Moscow (В. Мариньо [Mos.ru], 1995).

The Great Russia–India Connection

When I was at university, I went on a trip to Russia. At the time, it was known as the Union of Soviet Socialist Republics (USSR). I tried to learn a few Russian words and I found that the Russian phrase for 'goodbye' is '*dos vidaynya*'. '*Viday*' in Sanskrit also means taking leave. If you look a bit deeper into any completely foreign language, it begins to make sense that Sanskrit is the mother of Indo-European languages. Who would have thought that the word 'Thames' (as in the River Thames) is a word of Sanskrit origin? The Celtic people called it Tamesis, and there is a similarly named tributary of the Ganges, the Tamas, which means dark in Sanskrit. In Kenya, the rallying cry for a great joint effort is '*harambe*'. It is actually '*haar Ambe*', which was said when trying to accomplish a difficult task. Amba is a Hindu goddess. Though the Swahili language is not of Indo-European origin, it has a lot of Sanskrit-origin words due to the Hindu presence there.

The connection between Russia and India is not 5,000 years old, nor 10,000 years old, rather it is tens of thousands of years old.

The highest mountain in the Urals was called Narada by the local population. Narada is the most famous Hindu saint, who had the power to travel everywhere, including to different planets. On the 10th anniversary of the October Revolution of 1917, geologists decided to mark the event and rename the mountain Mount Narodnaya – meaning People's Mountain – and that's what it is now called in all geographic references and on all maps.

Narada was the guru of the young prince Prahalad, whose father was the demon Hiranyakashipu. Hiranyakashipu hated Prahalad for believing in god. He asked his sister Holika, who had a boon that she would never get burnt, to enter into a fire with the child Prahalad. Instead of Prahalad getting burnt, Holika got burnt. This event is celebrated by Hindus as the festival of Holi.

The Russian festival of Maslenitsa, which is also known as Butter Week, is the oldest surviving Slavic carnival. It is a seven-day festival with a striking similarity to the festival of Holi. On the last day, people ask for each other's forgiveness. Just as Holika was burnt in the fire, Lady Maslenitsa (in the form of a doll) is burnt in a bonfire.

According to the official website of Indradyumna Swami (1996), the following is what Alexander Vasilyevich Medvedev of the State University of Urals, Russia, said to the swami on 29th October 1996:

> *'The problem among our leaders,' he said, 'may not so much be in having to accept your movement but to accept the fact that the Vedic culture could have very well been the original culture here in Russia. You know, in Russia practically all scientists accept that the Vedic culture once flourished here, the centre being in the Volga River region. The debate among our scientists is only if the Aryans came from India or if they originated here. There is much evidence to the fact that the Vedic culture existed here, most notably the* Russian Veda.*'*
>
> *'The* Russian Veda?*' I asked.*
>
> *'Yes,' he said. 'It is famous among our people. It is as old as Russia, and the stories are exactly like those found in the Vedic scriptures. The central figure of the* Russian Veda *is a personality called Krishen. He is the upholder of spiritual truth and the killer of many demons. His killing of a witch and a snake are exactly like the history of child Krsna killing the Putanu and Agasura demons in the* Bhagavata Purana. *But the* Russian Veda *is not intended for children. It is full of spiritual truths.'*

That it was the Indians, then known as Aryans, who had settled in many parts of the world is now beyond doubt.

According to Knapp (2009), 'The discovery in 2007 of an ancient Vishnu sculpture dated 7th to 10th century in an excavation in Russia only confirms certain ideas I have always had about the Vedic ancient and glorious land and culture.'

The area in which the sculpture was found is called Staraya Maina. In the *Rig Veda*, there is a passage that reads '*Itham ascati pasyat syantham, ekam starayath mainaa-kaalam*.' This translates into 'Staraya Maina is the name of the land of the 45 rivers [on whose banks the noble rishis conducted the famous horse sacrifices], where the sun god descends into one fifty-two forty-seven.' While the first line identifies a location, the second line talks about the exact latitude and longitude at which the solar spectrum produces interference lines: 1, 52 and 47. The extreme precision of the calculations show the advanced science of the Vedic period, and that they had a thorough knowledge of SI units (it has been conclusively proven that French scientists stole the system from the Indians.)

The discovery of the sculpture confirms the location in Russia, identified in the *Rig Veda* as '*Rus Soviath sapthamahanagaratham*' (meaning the ancient and holy land of the 722 flying vehicles). The ancient connections between the Russians and the Indians has been unequivocally confirmed.

In Russian Orthodox Christianity, worship is conducted very much like in a Hindu temple.

According to Bulgarian linguist Vladimir Georgiev, geographical names are the most important source for determining how a group of people acquired their ethnicity. This can originate through a process of self-identification or it could be the result of outside identification. Georgiev confirms that the most stable – or longstanding – names are those of rivers, and furthermore, 'But in order to preserve the names it is necessary to maintain the continuity of the population, transmitting these names from generation to generation. Otherwise, new people may come and give it their own name' (Simha, 2014).

Russian scientist and academician A I Sobolewski (Simha, 2014) provides a list of Russian water bodies with Sanskrit names: 'Vaja (from *vaja* – strength), Valga (from *valgu* – simple), Ira (a refreshing drink), Karak (*karaka* – water jar), Cala (black), Lala (*lal* – play), Padma (lotus), Punk (silt), Sagara (ocean), Sarah (*sara* – juice), Sukhona (*suhana* – easy) and Harina (goose).'

Vyasa, Moksha, Kama, Nara and Siva are other river names of Sanskrit origin. Moskva is the Russian name for Moscow. Moscow is situated on the banks of Moskva River. '*Moksa*' is a Sanskrit word meaning liberation.

The Russian word ending of '*gorod*', meaning city, has a Sanskrit origin. In ancient times, cities were built to serve as forts for protection and defence. The Sanskrit word for fort is '*gadh*'. In modern Russian the suffix '*-grad*' and in modern Hindi the suffix '*-ghad*' are used to form names of cities such as Leningrad (the city of Lenin) or Chandigadh (city of the goddess Chandi).

When was the last time you had a shot of vodka? Well, next time you have one, remember that this Russian word has its origins in the Vedic Sanskrit word for water – '*udaka*'!

Here are more common words in Russian and Sanskrit:

Russian	**Sanskrit**	**English**
Naš	*Nas*	Ours
Svoi	*Sva*	One's own
Ty	*Tvam*	Thou
Dever	*Dever*	Brother-in-law
Grabit'	*Grabi*	To seize, loot
Myaso	*Mansa*	Animal flesh
Zhizn'	*Jivana*	Life
Nebo	*Nabhas*	Sky
Veter	*Vata*	Wind
Gora	*Giri*	Mountain
Bog	*Bhaga*	God

Russian	Sanskrit	English
Pochitaniye	*Puja*	Worship
Noch	*Nakta*	Night
Ogon	*Agni*	Fire
Dver	*Dvara*	Door
Soyuz	*Samyoga*	Union
Znana	*Jnana*	Knowledge
Topit	*Tapati*	To warm
Vseda	*Sada*	Always
Mgla	*Megha*	Cloud

These are some Russian and Sanskrit phrases of striking similarity:

Russian	Sanskrit	English
Eto nash dom	*Etas nath dham*	My house
Aeto seen tat	*Dham seenu*	My son's house
Etat dom snokhi	*Etat dham snukhi*	My daughter-in-law's house

According to Simha (2014):

> *The two languages have two broad similarities. One, Russian is the only European language that shares a strong common grammatical base with Sanskrit. Secondly, both Russian and Sanskrit are pleasing to the ear. The very name 'Sanskrit' means carefully constructed, systematically formed, polished and refined. Colonial era linguist William Jones wrote: 'Sanskrit language is of a wonder structure; more perfect than the Greek, more copious than the Latin and more exquisitely refined than either.'*

The uncanny similarities between Sanskrit and Russian clearly indicate that there was a close kinship between the two nations in the distant past. Russian Indologists have long been aware of this connection. In 1787, N I Novikov translated Charles Wilkins' rendition of the *Bhagavad Gita* from English to Russian.

It is stated that the style of the verse of Russian folk legends and Pushkin's tales are closer to the rhythm of Sanskrit verse. Professor Smirnov (1892–1967), the reputed Sanskritologist of the Soviet Union has translated the *Mahabharata* into Russian in this type of verse. Professor Smirnov had with him a recording of an extract from the *Mahabharata* read in the original Sanskrit by Professor Nirmal Chandra Maitra of India to the accompaniment of Indian instruments. After playing the recording of the Sanskrit version, Professor Smirnov read his Russian translation, and the enchanting melody of the rhythm was found to be very much like that of the original Sanskrit version as read by Professor Nirmal Chandra Maitra, and they sounded to be in unison.

The Russia–India connection does not end here. Counting in Russian begins *adin*, *dwa*, *tr*, *i*, *chitri*, *peyas*, *sheshtha*, etc. And in Sanskrit it goes *eka*, *dw*, *i*, *tri*, *chatur*, *pancha*, *shash*! Russians were well versed with the Indian counting system, as is evident from the fact that Russian chemist and inventor, Dmitry Mendeleev, who gave the world the periodic law of elements and the famous Mendeleev periodic table in 1856, which uses the prefixes '*eka*', '*dvi*' and '*tri*' in naming his predicted eight elements. Noting that there are striking similarities between the periodic table and the introductory Siva Sutras in Panini's grammar, Ghosh and Kiparsky (2019) said 'The analogies between the two systems are striking. Just as Panini found that the phonological patterning of sounds in the language is a function of their articulatory properties, so Mendeleev found that the chemical properties of elements are a function of their atomic weights.'

This same article by Ghosh and Kiparsky (2019) also states the following:

> *The importance of Sanskrit to the study of linguistics and European languages was already well-known to European philologists and linguists at that time. They knew that Sanskrit is linguistically related to the great majority of modern European languages (with the exception of Finnish, Basque, and a handful of others) as well as Farsi (but not Turkish and Arabic).*

> *To us, Mendeleev's remarkable use of the Sanskrit numerals eka-, dvi-, and tri- in naming as yet undiscovered elements makes the most sense as an homage to Panini, not only to his periodic alphabet, but also more generally to his generative, combinatorial approach to language. Mendeleev presumably saw this approach as analogous to his own quest for a grammar of nature. One of the most iconic symbols of modern science, as it arose in the latter part of the 19th century in Europe, may thus owe a significant debt to an ancient Eastern language and culture.*

According to Ghosh and Kiparsky (2019), what Panini did for Sanskrit, Mendeleev tried to do for chemistry.

Leo Tolstoy (1828–1910) – Russia's great philosopher, novelist and playwright – was also influenced by Buddhism and Hinduism. He endorsed the Buddhist concepts of karma and reincarnation. He was familiar with the *Vedas* and *Upanishads* as well as the *Ramayana* and *Mahabharata*. He was also a committed vegetarian. Conversely, Leo Tolstoy greatly influenced Mahatma Gandhi. Gandhi took the idea of non-violent passive resistance from Tolstoy and used it successfully both in South Africa and India. He also started his ashram, which was called Tolstoy Farm, in Johannesburg based on Tolstoy's ideas. It was from there that the Satyagraha struggle was fought between 1908 and 1914.

Hinduism in Present-Day Russia

Srila Prabhupada, the founder of the Hare Krishna Society, laid the foundations of the movement in Russia during his visit to Moscow in 1971. At the time, Russia was in the solid grip of communism and militant atheism. Despite that, Srila Prabhupada managed to sow the seeds of Sanatan Dharma. Today, tens of thousands of Russians are Hare Krishna devotees. Thousands of Russians travel to the holy city of Vrindavan in India every year.

There are many other Hindu groups active in Russia. Temples may open in areas of Russia where there was a big Hindu influence in the distant past!

The Great Slavic and Balkan Countries–India Connection

The group of Slavic nations comprises the following countries: Belarus, Russia, Ukraine (the eastern part only), Czech Republic, Poland, Slovakia (the western part only), Albania, Bosnia and Herzegovina, Bulgaria, Romania, Croatia, North Macedonia, Montenegro, Serbia and Slovenia (the southern part only) (with those countries listed from Albania onwards also being part of the Balkan states).

By the beginning of the 19th century, the Slavic people were under either the Austrian or Russian empire. In a bid to find their own identity, they turned towards India, especially with respect to literary and linguistic aspects. It did not take them long to discover striking similarities between the Slavic countries and India.

The Sanskrit word '*veda*', meaning knowledge, has the same meaning in the Czech, Slovak and Polish languages.

According to James Cooper (2015):

> *For most of the Croatian people (or as they call themselves, Hrvati) when it comes to defining their origins and tracing their ancient roots they turn towards the land of Iran and Persia. According to academia the name Hrvat... is ultimately traced to Persia and the name Harahvaiti.*
>
> *Harahvaiti, however, is the corrupted name of Sarasvati, the great Vedic Goddess, the Mother of Sanskrit, the great river of the* Rig Veda *and the Goddess of learning. The Persians had a tendency to replace a Sanskrit 'S' with a Persian 'H', and so the word Haravaiti is actually Sarasvati.*

He further says this:

Istra is a magical region of Croatia, known as Terra Magica, 'the magic land'. Its name comes from an equally magical source known as the Illyrians, an Indo/European civilisation who populated these lands some 4000 years ago. The regions of Istra, their islands and surrounding area, all the way to north-eastern area known as Slavonia, and down the Dalmatian coast, read like a page from a Sanskrit dictionary – Rupa – Raša – Rukavac – Kršan – Sukošan – Daruvar – Kali – Duga Uvala – Duga Resa – Isa – Siverić – Nos Kalik – Kalinić – Kalinovac – Budimir – Rajakovići – Kuje – Sava – Budva – Dvigrad – Ruda – Rava – Mandal – Radovani – Loka – Bogdanov Vrh – Predloka – Radoboj – Sveta Nedelja – Sit – Štanjel – Antignana – Grisignana – Galignana – Lisignana – Dignano – Visignano – Hvar.

Spotted in isolation, they would deserve nothing more than a raised eyebrow, but seeing a number of them, and taking into consideration the similarity between the Croatian and Sanskrit languages, we can only conclude that at some time in the distant past there was a presence of Vedic India in those lands.

Cooper (2015) also notes how Sanskrit words have made their way into people's names:

In Sanskrit we have the word Sveta which means 'light', 'bright', 'white'...

From the Sanskrit Sveta we get the Croatian first names: Sveta or Svjetlana or Sveto – all of them pertaining to 'light', 'bright' and by extension 'pure' or 'saintly'.

(In many other Slavic nations we get the variations of the same word, so in Russia for example, we have Svetlana, in Czechoslovakia Svetla and in Bulgaria its Svetul.)

> *... Throughout Croatia we see this Sanskrit sveta in many place names such as Sveta Marija – Sveta Nedelja – Sveti Durd – Sveti Ivan – Sveti Juraj – Sveti Lovrec – Sveti Martin – Sveti Peter – Svetvinčenat.*

Cooper (2015) also describes how the Sanskrit word '*jnana*', meaning knowledge, is the source of the Greek word '*gnosis*', from which we ultimately get the English word 'knowledge'. The word with the meaning that is the opposite of knowledge is 'ignorance', which comes from the Sanskrit '*agnan*'. Cooper (2015) also notes how this word '*jnana*' has made its way into place names:

> *In Croatia, on the enchanted islands of Istra, there are regions which bear this very same name, jnana. There is Grisignana – Lisignana – Galignana – Antignana – Dignano and Visignano. We find little information on these places except they are very ancient having been inhabited for over 7,000 years.*
>
> *Kali is an island off the coast of Istra, the name is an obvious Vedic/Hindu name, yet here it is as an island of Croatia in a land whose language is hardly distinguishable from Sanskrit. Throughout the region we also find names such as Kalinovac, Kalik and Kalinić.*

Other names discussed by Cooper (2015) are the names of several rivers. Firstly, the Drava River, which has its source in Italy and flows through Austria, Slovenia, Croatia and Hungary. '*Draven*' is a Sanskrit word meaning stream. Another river is called the Raša, which in Sanskrit means liquid, juice, nectar, love and taste, among other things. Furthermore, Croatia also has a river called Sava, which means water pouring out in Sanskrit.

Staying with Croatia, Cooper (2015) also identifies a Croatian town named Bogdanov Vrh, meaning gift of god, which comes from the Sanskrit words '*bhaga*' (meaning god) and '*dan*' (meaning to give or gift). Bogdan and Bogdanovic are also popular Slavic names, where Bogdanovic means 'son of Bogdan'.

Cogniarchae (2016), a cognitive archaeological site, describes that there is a city called Indjija in Serbia. The Germans and Slovaks call it India. Near a place called Sanad in Serbia there is a place called Bogarsh; similarly, near the Indian city of Sanand in Gujarat there is a river called Bhagirath. Mount Athos of Serbia is known as Sveta Gora in Bulgaria, Macedonia and Serbia, and is called Svyataya Gora in Russia. All these names mean holy white mountain. The Hindu holy scripture of the *Srimad Bhagavatam* mentions an area known as Hiranmayavarsa. It is the abode of the supreme Lord Vishnu in his tortoise form. The principal mountain range there is the Sveta range, meaning white.

The *Rig Veda* mentions a tribe called Krivi, and one of the most important Slavic tribes of the sixth century had the same name: Krivich or Kryvich (Cogniarchae, 2019).

According to Cogniarchae (2016):

> *The Hinduistic concept of Moksha* [freedom from the cycle of birth and death] *and Svarga* [heaven] *mirrors in the names of deities in the Slavic pantheon – Mokosh and Svrog… The triple-headed god of the Indus Valley civilization later associated with Shiva, appears in Slavic mythology as Triglav* [meaning three-headed]… *On the other hand, the famous four-headed Zbruch idol from* [Poland] *matches perfectly depictions of Brahma.*

The Zbruch idol that Cogniarchae (2016) mentions is believed to be one of the rarest artefacts of the pre-Christian Slavic era. It is displayed in Krakow Archaeological Museum.

It is also explained by Cogniarchae (2016) that when Christianity reached Slavic lands in the ninth century, the Vedic gods were replaced with saints, such as Indra becoming St Andrew. Andrew is a non-Semitic, non-Hebrew name. Worship of St Andrew with his cross was widespread in early Britain and Ireland. The cross of St Andrew is simply a battleaxe or hammer, which is also the symbol of Indra. It represents Indra slaying the dragon of darkness and death. The goat is the favoured animal of Indra, the image of which can be seen on many coats of arms of European nations in the form of a unicorn. The Welsh Royal regiment has had a goat mascot since 1775. The ancient X cross of Indra is also seen on the British flag and many other flags. There are many folk traditions celebrated on St Andrew's Day (30th November) in the Slavic nations. One of them is that women looking for a good husband pray for one to St Andrew on that day. Conversely, in the *Rig Veda* 4, 17, 16, there are prayers to Lord Indra from men to grant them good wives! St Andrew, who is the patron saint of Scotland, is none other than the god Indra!

St Patrick of Ireland also carried a cross of Indra to create miracles. This was much before the cross was identified with the crucifix. St Demetrius, the horse-mounted saint, came into Christianity from the Hindu horse-mounted deity Mitra. He is revered by Bulgarians, Romanians, Serbians and Macedonians. His holy day is still celebrated by the name Mitrovdan or Mitra's Day.

Strangely, there have been two Slavic *Vedas* (Cogniarchae, 2016). One is called *Perun's Veda*, which was written in 26,731 BCE and then there is the *Slavic Veda*. They have profound knowledge covering a host of issues, including inter-planetary travel going back 600,000 years. There is mention of Hindu gods, such as Vishnu, in them. Of a compilation of 345 poems found in a Serbian monastery, 15 talk about the Indian origin of Serbia.

The ancient orthodox church of Russia and the Slavic people is called Ynglist ('Ynglism', 2021). According to the Ynglist calendar, the first month – which falls in September and October – is called Ramah or Ramkha. Ramah is considered to be the supreme lord. A hymn in his praise is as follows:

Great Ramha, one supreme creator,
You are in all worlds, giving them life!
We glorify you, in all our nations, temples and sanctuaries,
In all our settlements, cities and villages,
In all sacred groves and in all oaks,
On the banks of the sacred rivers and lakes;

For holy Yngly, that brings to us the light of love and joy,
And illuminates our hearts and thoughts.
Let all our deeds be done, for your glory,
Now and ever from circle to circle.
The symbol of the Ynglist church is a swastika.

Lepenski Vir in Serbia is the oldest prehistoric site in Europe. It dates from 9,500 BCE. During an excavation, they found a skeleton in the lotus or Padmasana posture. It has baffled archaeologists!

The two-headed eagle is on the national flags of Albania, Montenegro and Serbia; is on the coat of arms of Russia and Croatia; and is also the symbol of the Orthodox Christian Churches in Slavic countries. It is a symbol of great strength. The Puranas (Indian legends) mention that, after killing the demon Hiranyakashipu, Lord Vishnu appeared as a two-headed eagle to fight Lord Shiva, who was in his form of Sharabha a powerful eight-legged beast.

A Maharaja Creates a Special Bond Between Poland and India

According to the Polish History Museum (n.d.), as the Second World War raged, Poland was trapped between Lenin's Russia and Hitler's Germany. Hundreds of Polish children were orphaned. Maharaja Digvijaysinhji Ranjit Singhji of Nawanagar, near Jamnagar, Gujarat, India, came to know about it and offered to host them. In 1942, around 600 Polish children, some of them Jewish, made the hazardous journey by sea and land from Siberia. On the way, they were denied entry from all ports from Iran to Mumbai, which was under British rule at that time. When they at last arrived at Nawanagar, the maharaja welcomed them personally and said, 'You are no longer orphans. From now on you are Nawangarians, and I am Bapu, father of all Nawangarians, so I'm your father as well.' The age range of the children was two to seventeen. The malnourished and unwell children were given great medical care. An Indian doctor, Asham, learnt Polish to be able to understand the health issues of the children. The maharaja offered the guest rooms of his palace to be used as a school for the children. The children were provided with many activities, including sports and other outdoor activities. Businesses such as Tata and many individuals raised over 600,000 rupees for the welfare of the children. It was a huge amount at the time. A chapel and a Catholic priest were provided to meet the spiritual needs of the children. Special care was taken to teach the children about their cultural heritage. The Polish government gave Maharaja Digvijaysinhji the Cross of the Order of Merit of the Republic of Poland posthumously.

Another refugee centre for older people was set up in Valivade near Kolhapur, Maharashtra, India. Between 1942 and 1948, there were 5,000 Polish refugees there. Over a period of six years, some 20,000 refugees from many nationalities passed through the centre. A square in Warsaw, Poland, is named after the maharaja, and a small park in Warsaw's Ochita area is also called the Square of the Good Maharaja. The Friends of India Education Foundation in Warsaw runs schools in Bednarska and Baszynska Street, which keep the arts and artefacts of India as a reminder of the refugee children who spent time in India. The school also provides free food for the refugees in the city. This event is a proud chapter in India's history, which saved the lives of hundreds of children.

The Romany Connection

The Romany people, also known as Gypsies, are a people who left India between the 8th and 10th centuries. They live in Serbia, Romania, Croatia, Moldova, Bulgaria, North Macedonia, Hungary, Slovakia and Ukraine. In Romania, Bulgaria, North Macedonia, Hungary and Ukraine, they are a very large minority. They brought with them music, dance, palmistry and craftsmanship. They were blacksmiths, cobblers, tinsmiths and tool makers, as well as horse dealers. The Romany language is based on Hindi. The Spanish flamenco dance has Romany origins, which in turn comes from the Indian classical dance form Kathak.

Present-Day Slavic Countries and India

There is huge interest in Slavic countries regarding many aspects of Indian life, including India's classical dance forms, music, yoga and much more. Hinduism is the third largest religion in Russia, and in many other Slavic countries there are Hare Krishna temples and Krishna country farms. Many Hindu schools of thought have a presence in these countries. Tens of thousands of devotees from these countries go to India to visit places such as Vrindavan. The Slavic and Indian peoples, who have ancient connections, are reconnecting, with Sanskrit as the common denominator!

Hanuman statue, Honduras (Eichmann, 1980). CC BY-SA 4.0.

The Great Mayan Empire–India Connection

Former US ambassador to Peru, Miles Poindexter (1868–1946) called the Mayan civilisation 'unquestionably Hindu' (Poindexter, 1930).

World-leading anthropologists Robert von Heine-Geldern (1885–1968) and Gordon F. Ekholm (1909–1987) strongly support the claim that Indian ships went all the way to Mexico and Peru centuries before Columbus. In the paper *The Civilizations of Ancient America*, they state the following (1951, cited in Lal, 1968, pp. 43–44):

> *There appears to be little doubt but that ship building and navigation were sufficiently advanced in southern and eastern Asia at the period in question to have made trans-Pacific voyages possible. In the third century, horses were exported from India to the Malay Peninsula and Indo-China, an indication that there must have been ships of considerable size.*

A closer look at the ancient Mayan civilisation in Mexico, as well as the Inca and Aztec civilisations, reveals an amazing similarity with the thoughts and beliefs that have flowed in India for thousands of years.

Indians were master navigators and seafarers. They were probably the first settlers in the Americas. The word '*catamaran*', meaning the type of boat or ship on which Indians sailed to the Americas, is the same in Spanish.

The Mayan civilisation, which covered Guatemala, Honduras, Belize, El Salvador and the Yucatán province of Mexico, has great similarities with Hindu legends and beliefs. The Mayans could well have been Hindu seafarers who settled in these countries.

In 1949, two scholars – Gordon Ekholm and Chaman Lal – systematically compared the Maya, Aztec, Inca and North American indigenous civilisations with India and the Hindu-Buddhist-oriented countries of Southeast Asia. They found signs of Hindu civilisation throughout the Americas, in art, architecture, calendars, astronomy, religious symbols, etc. The zenith of the Mayan civilisation was reached at a time when ancient India had attained an unparalleled cultural peak during the Gupta Period in 320 CE.

In his book *Hindu America*, Chaman Lal (1940) covers many of the topics discussed in the following paragraphs.

Like the Hindus in India, the Mayan people believed that the gods/goddesses of earth, water, wind and fire (Prithvi, Jal, Vayu and Agni, respectively, in the Hindu pantheon) were the source of human life. The Mayans worshipped the sun god, the moon god, the rain god (Surya, Chandra and Indra, respectively, in the Hindu pantheon), and many other gods and goddesses.

The Mayan temples also have images of elephants and other animals. There have never been elephants on the American continent, so the question remains as to how they came to be carved on the Mayan temples. The phallic symbol of Lord Shiva is also carved on most temples, and they have also been found in many places throughout America. The swastika has also been found in many Mayan ruins.

A stone sculpture of Lord Hanuman exists in Honduras. According to Douglas Preston (2015), a lost city of a monkey god has been found in the dense forests of Mosquitia, Honduras. It could possibly put a spotlight on an entire pre-Columbian civilisation.

On the border of Honduras, in the autonomous region of Nicaragua is a town called Rama, and there is also a river by the same name. An image of Hanuman, which is called Huemana, has also been found in Guatemala. In a temple in Guatemala, there is a statue of a tortoise, which is an incarnation of Vishnu. Small tortoise structures can also be found on the ground at many Mayan sites.

I have personally seen stone sculptures on Mayan monuments in Mexico that are replicas of Hindu goddesses.

According to Aria Nuova (n.d.):

> *The history of pre-Columbian America is obscure because after the Spanish conquest, the first Bishop of Mexico, Juan de Zumarraga, burned all the records of the Library of Texcoco in Tlatelolco market square as 'the work of the Devil', and religious fanatics destroyed temples and statues. Zumarraga, gloating over his success, wrote to his superiors in 1531 that he alone had destroyed five hundred replicas of Hindu goddesses. The Hindu lotus and chakra motifs adorn Mayan temples razed to the ground and twenty thousand idols destroyed.*
>
> *Fray Diego de Landa, the second Bishop of Yucatan, following the pattern, reduced the Maya Library in Yucatan to ashes in 1562. Post-Columbus history of America for 300 years was the story of ruthless destruction and fanatics like Bishop Diego da Landa burnt a huge bonfire of valuable documents and nothing but the three codices of 'Chilam Balam' could survive the holocaust. He wrote* Relación de las cosas de Yucatán, A Narrative of the Things of Yucatán *in 1566, therein he states, 'We found a large number of their books of these letters, and because they did not have anything in which there was not superstition and falsehoods of the devil, we burned them all, which they felt very sorry for and which caused them grief'* (Proof [of] Vedic Culture's Global Existence – *By Stephen Knapp [2009]).*
>
> *Landa, in his religious zeal, ordered all their idols destroyed and all Mayan books to be burned; he was surprised at the distress this caused the Indians. His orders to destroy all icons and hieroglyphics obliterated the Mayan language forever, helping to undermine and destroy the civilization he so vividly described.*

It was Landa that gave the orders for all the Mayans to bring all manuscripts to the public squares in Mani to be burned. All these books contained what would now be priceless information on astronomy, medicine, religion, and philosophy. What Emperor Theodosious of Constantinople did to the library at Alexandria to save Christianity from the Greek and Oriental pagan knowledge deposited there, these priests did in Central America with similar motives but larger success.

The burning of manuscripts continued for decades. Soldiers were encouraged to ransack palaces, public buildings, and private houses to find manuscripts. Pablo Jose de Arriaga, the head of the Jesuit College in Peru, in almost unparalleled fanaticism, caused the systematic and wholesale destruction of all state archives, customs records, royal and imperial archives, codes of laws, temple archives, and historical records. Less than a score of manuscripts escaped annihilation. These libraries contained records of ancient history, medicine, astronomy, science, religion, and philosophy.

Beyond Mexico, the ancient Andean or Peruvian civilization also suffered an even worse fate at the hands of the Spaniards than did their neighbours in Central America. The Spanish assault on the Incas, the Spanish avarice of gold, and barbarities perpetrated in the wake of victory, including the inhuman tortures publicly inflicted on the Inca King, Atahualpa, are illustrations of savagery seldom surpassed in history [. . .]

The Devastation of the Indies *written by Bartholome de Las Casas* [states], 'The Devastation of the Indies *is an eyewitness account of the first modern genocide, a story of greed, hypocrisy, and cruelties so grotesque as to rival the worst of our own century'. Las Casas writes of men, women and children burned alive "thirteen at a time in memory of Our Redeemer and his twelve apostles".'*

It is estimated that, during the colonial period (1492–1832), a total of 1.86 million Spaniards settled in the Americas and a further 3.5 million immigrated during the post-colonial era (1850–1950). By contrast, the indigenous population plummeted by an estimated 80 per cent in the first one and a half centuries following Columbus's voyages, primarily through the spread of disease, forced labour, slavery and missionary work. It was a truly dark period in history.

In the year 1786, Sir William Jones – an Anglo –Welsh philologist and a scholar of ancient India who was particularly known for his proposition of the existence of a relationship among European and Indo-Aryan languages – found the imprints of the stories of Rama and Sita in the remnants of the Mayan civilisation:

> *Rama is represented as a descendant from the sun. He was the husband of Sita and the son of a princess named Causelya. It is very remarkable that Peruvians, whose Inces boasted the same descent, styled their greatest festival – Rama-Sitva, whence we may suppose that South America was peopled by the same race who imported into the farthest parts of Asia, the rites and the fabulous history of Ram.* (Jones, 1884, p. 426)

Professor Ramon Mena, curator of the National Museum of Mexico, stated that the Nahuati or Mexicano language spoken in central Mexico, the Zapotec language spoken by the Zapotec people, and the Mayan languages spoken in Guatemala, Mexico, Belize, El Salvador and Honduras are of 'Hindu origin' (Mena, 1924).

The Spanish author Lopez (1871) writes 'Every page of Peruvian poetry bears the imprint of *Ramayana* and *Mahabharata*.'

The word 'Aztec' could be derived from meaning one who worships Ashtabhuja or Ashtak, who is the eight-armed god found in Mexican temples. The only other place where a multi-armed god is worshipped is India.

The Mayans were also primarily vegetarian, as Hindus are. Mexican tortillas are very similar to Indian rotis or chapatis. Cotton was most probably introduced to South America by the Indians.

There could be an even older connection between India and the Americas. The *Surya Siddhanta* is the oldest surviving astronomical text in the Indian tradition. It explains that the earth is shaped like a ball, and that at the very opposite side of the planet from India there is a great city where the sun is rising at the same time as it sets in India. In this city, the *Surya Siddhanta* claims, lives a race of Siddhas or advanced spiritual beings. If you trace round the globe to the exact opposite side from India, you will find Mexico. This means that Indians were aware of the Americas tens of thousands of years ago.

Looking at the present, is it not strange that followers of the same beliefs are now residing in their millions in North America, and they are building new temples?

Knowing what we know of the enterprising skills of the Indian community, it is quite possible that there might be some, if not many, of them moving on to Central America and, eventually, temples will open that are not far from the ancient temples of the Mayan people!

The Great Ancient Egypt–India Connection

(This chapter incorporates the Indian influence in other Middle Eastern countries and East Africa).

Louis Jacolliot (1837–1890) – a barrister, author and government official in French India – stated that 'No one could contest the purely Hindu origin of Egypt.'

Sir William Jones (1746–1794), a scholar of ancient India, said the following:

> *Of the cursory observations of the Hindus, which it would require volumes to expand and illustrate, this is the result: that they have an immortal affinity with the old Persians, Ethiopians, Egyptians, Phoenicians, Greeks, Tuscans, to the Scythians or Goths and Celts, the Chinese, Japanese and Peruvians.*

The Phoenicians were seafaring people from parts of what is now modern Lebanon, Syria and northern Israel. The Scythians or Goths were originally from southern Siberia. They flourished between 900 BCE and 200 BCE. During this time, they extended their influence all over Central Asia from China to the Black Sea.

Doshi (1993) gives a comprehensive account of the Indian origin of Egyptian civilisation. The *Skanda Purana* is called *Egypt Sancha-Dvipa*. (*Puranas* are ancient Indian histories.)

According to both Dio Chrysostom (100 CE) and Clement (200 CE), Indian scholars were a common sight in Alexandria.

The name Egypt comes from the shortened term 'Ajap', which refers to the Sanskrit name Ajapati. Aja was the grandfather of Lord Rama.

Dr Gordon Childe (1892–1957), an Australian archaeologist, explained that 'In the third millennium BC India was already in a position to contribute to the building up of the cultural traditions that constitute Egypt's spiritual heritage as she notoriously has done since the time of Alexander the Great.'

Paul William Roberts (2007), a Canadian writer, said this:

> *Recent research and scholarship make it increasingly possible to believe that the Vedic era was the lost civilization whose legacy the Egyptians and the Indians inherited. There must have been one. There are too many similarities between hieroglyphic texts and Vedic ones.*

Johann Peter Adolf Erman (1854–1937), a professor of Egyptology at Berlin University, maintains that 'Egyptian legends make it clear that people from a place called Punt, believed to be India, laid the foundation stone of their civilisation. Punt could be the shortened version of Pundit.'

Heinrich Karl Brugsch (1827–1894), arguably the greatest Egyptologist in the 19th century, quotes Egyptologist Bengsch Bey, who stated 'We have a right to more than suspect that India, eight thousand years ago, sent a colony of emigrants who carried their arts and high civilisation into what is now Egypt' (Brugsch, 1879).

Edward Pocoke (1604–1691), an English orientalist said this:

> *At the mouth of the Indus dwell a seafaring people, active, ingenious and enterprising as when, ages subsequent to this great movement—these people found the kingdom of Egypt, these are the same people that centuries subsequently to this colonisation, spread the blessings of civilisation over Hellas and her islands.* (Pocoke, 1852)

The Greeks were known as Hella or Hellenic before they came under the Christian empire of Byzantine.

Arnold Hermann Ludwig Heeren (1760–1842), a German historian and Egyptologist, stated 'It is perfectly agreeable to Hindu manners that colonies from India, i.e. Banian families should have passed over Africa and carried with them their industry and perhaps also their religious worship' (Heeren, 1833).

Herodotus (who is known as the 'Father of History'), Plato, Salon, Pythagoras and Philostratus all believed that the religion of Egypt proceeded from India. It is testified by Neibhur, Valentia, Champollan and Weddington that the temples of Upper Egypt are of greater antiquity than those of Lower Egypt, and that, consequently, according to the testimony of those monuments, the religion of Egypt came from India.

Significant Similarities Between the Egyptian and Hindu Cultures

The Egyptians had four castes just like the four Hindu *jatis*.

Egyptian kings, like Hindu kings, had two names: one given at birth and one given on their coronation.

There are many things that are commonly worshipped in both India and Egypt, such as the cow, snake, sun and river. Cows are sacred in India, and the Egyptian goddess Hathor is often represented by a cow and is considered very sacred. Just as Hindus worship the River Ganges, the Egyptians used to worship the River Nile; Hapi is the god of the River Nile. The word 'Nile' is believed to be of Sanskrit origin; it comes from the word '*nil*', which means blue.

The lotus flower is associated with the goddess Lakshmi. It also had huge significance in Egypt.

The soul is often seen as a bird in Ancient Egyptian literature. In the *Upanishads*, the soul and the super soul are compared with birds. One bird is eating (which is the soul) and the other one is watching (which is the super soul). The super soul notes the actions of the soul or *atma*.

The Hindu swastika can also be found on Egyptian drawings.

Just like the Egyptian pharaohs were preserved, the *Srimad Bhagvatam* gives the story of King Nimi, whose body was preserved. The great sages and saints asked the demigods to revive King Nimi. The demigods had the power to revive a dead body.

They both have a tradition of breaking vessels. Hindus used to break all mud pots, have a bath and change their clothes after a funeral. This was to remove all negative energies. The Egyptians did the same. The Egyptian *Book of the Dead* and the *Garuda Purana* are similar and are recited at the time of death.

The Sphinx and the Purusha Mriga (or Purusha Mruga) are similar. The Sphinx has the head of a human and the body of a lion. Sometimes it also has the wings of a bird. This is also true of the Purusha Mriga, which was a renowned devotee of Lord Shiva. It can be seen on the walls of Hindu temples as well as on lamps in Tamil Nadu.

Many Egyptian kings or pharaohs had the name Rameses. An emperor of Memphis in northern Egypt is shown with a Vaishnava *tilak* or mark on the forehead. This indicates that they were descendants of Lord Rama.

The Pyramids Connection

K. Sennaya Swamy Muthukrishnan is an Indian Egyptologist who is best known for discovering that the base triangles of the Egyptian pyramids of Giza are equal in angular measurements to those of the Sri Yantra (which is a 10,000-year-old mystical geometrical figure). He believed that the pyramids are not tombs, but are giant instruments that were used to harness cosmic energy for practical purposes.

According to Vedavyas (1995):

> *Sri Yantra Sutra's 3 dimensional geometric pattern contains the elusive theory of everything (TOE). The golden ratio from the mystic Vaastu geometry of Sri Yantra of Indian Vedic times 10,000 years ago was 51 des, 49 minutes, 38.25 seconds. They are the angle measurements of both the Egyptian pyramids and the Sri Yantra.*

Vaastu is an Indian system of scientific architecture that takes into account earth, water, fire and wind to balance cosmic energies.

The Data Encryption Standard (DES) algorithm is a block cipher, which means that it operates on plaintext blocks of a given size (64-bits) and returns ciphertext blocks of the same size.

Indian Influence in Other Parts of the Middle East

According to Pocoke (1852)(1604–1691), an English orientalist, 'The word Persia is from the Sanskrit word Parsuram the legendary fighter. The people of Persia were from Bharat (India). The principal stream that pours waters into the Persian Gulf is known as Eu-Bharat-Es (Euphrates).'

The Persians later changed their faith to Zoroastrianism. Interestingly, Zoroastrians have a collection of 21 hymns called *Yasht*. *Yasht* number 15 is called 'Ram Yasht'. It offers prayers to Lord Rama.

By a strange coincidence, the same Zoroastrians or Parsis left Persia and took refuge in India due to religious persecution in around the 10th century.

Indian fables, legends and literature also made their way to the West and into the Middle East as early as the sixth century BCE. The Buddhist *Jatakas*, Vedic *Panchatantra* and the *Hitopadesha* were translated into Persian under the name of *Jutinamah*. These stories found their way to Europe. The story of 'Two Jackals, Karakatak and Damanaka' was translated into Persian, Syriac, Latin, Hebrew and Spanish. All these fables were woven into the very fabric of European literature.

The *Jataka Tales* are stories of Lord Buddha's previous incarnations. Up to 50 per cent of all nursery rhymes and ballads are from the *Jataka Tales*. The *Hitopadesh* (meaning good-advice stories) were written in the 12th century by Narayana. *Panchatantra* are five treatises attributed to Vishnu Sharma, dated 300 BCE. They are a collection of animal fables that teach children good moral values and wise conduct in life. These stories have circulated worldwide and are considered most famous. There are 200 versions of the *Panchatantra* in more than 50 languages throughout the world.

According to Walt Whitman (1819–1892), an American poet and essayist, *Kalilah and Dimnah*, the Arabian book of fables, has been translated from the *Panchatantra*.

Many Western nursery rhymes are based on the *Panchatantra* stories. The *Panchatantra* has influenced 90 to 96 human generations. Giovanni Boccaccio (1313–1375), Italian writer and poet, and Geoffrey Chaucer (1343–1400), who is considered to be the greatest English poet of the Middle Ages, were influenced by the style and structure of the *Panchatantra*. In addition to yoga and vegetarianism, the *Panchatantra* is another gift of India to the world!

A king named Dashrath ruled over Syria and Iraq 3,000 years ago. It was then known as the kingdom of Mittani. They worshipped the Hindu gods called Mitra, Varuna, Indra and Nasatya. (The twin gods of Ashwini Kumars are known as Nasatya and Dasra. They are sons of the sun god.) The word 'Syria' comes from Surya the sun god.

The Sumerians were probably the oldest known residents of the Middle East. Sir Arthur Keith (1866–1955) said that Sumerians were part of the Vedic tradition (Knapp, 2018). Also, a book called *The Sumerians*, an Oxford publication (Knapp, 2018), says 'archaeological evidence in the form of relics of the Sumerian language still exists which leaves no doubt as to the real incentive behind the origins of the Sumerian language'.

The Druze people live mainly in Lebanon and Israel, but also in some other countries in the Middle East. Their late leader Kamal Jumblatt (1917–1977) often glorified Krishna, the *Bhagavad Gita*, the *Ramayana* and other Hindu scriptures. He was a vegetarian, and in his later years, he lived according to the Hindu Vanprastha stage. (The Vanprastha stage is when one gives up all material desires and concentrates on god consciousness). He travelled to India and found a guru. The Druze people believe in reincarnation; their scriptures describe a history going back millions of years, with incarnations of gods appearing in human form regularly, just as in Hinduism.

The persecuted Yazidi people of Iraq also have many traditions with similarities to Hinduism. The peacock is revered in both cultures. The Yazidi perform prayers with lighted lamps just as the Hindus do in the Aarti ceremony. They fold their hands in prayer. Yazidis marry only within their own castes. They have four castes just like the four Hindu *jatis*. They believe in reincarnation. Circumcision is not considered obligatory for Yazidis. They wear a mark on their forehead while entering their temples, which is similar to a *bindi* or *tilak*. (Hindus have the concept of a third eye. One can activate the third eye, which is situated between the two eyebrows. A person who can activate their third eye becomes a seer, who is able to foresee things, hence the name.)

Fire worship is given the highest priority in Yazidi worship, which is similar to Havan in the Vedic tradition.

Yazidi temples are constructed like Hindu temples.

Jain temple, Mombasa. White monumental building with columns (Reitveld, 1975). CC BY-SA 4.0.

Magnificent Sikh temple in Makindu, Kenya, built by Sikh railway workers in 1926 (HiraV, 2016). CC BY-SA 4.0.

The Great East Africa–India Connection

John Hanning Speke (1827–1864), when planning his discovery of the source of the Nile, secured his best information from a map reconstructed from the *Puranas*. The conventional wisdom was that Lake Tanganyika was the source of the Nile. However, a Hindu *pundit* (or *pandit*) from Banaras (also known as Varanasi) told Speke that the real source was a much larger lake that lay to the north. Following his advice, Speke went on to discover Lake Victoria. The *pundit* had also told Speke that the real source were twin peaks known as Somagiri. '*Soma*' in Sanskrit means the moon, and '*giri*' means peak. Therefore, Somagiri are none other than the fabled Mountains of the Moon in Central Africa. According to Speke, it is remarkable that the Hindus have christened the source of the Nile 'Amara'. '*Amara*' in Sanskrit means immortal, and there was a country by that name in the north-east corner of the Victoria Nyanza. ('*Nyanza*' in the Bantu language means a large mass of water; Bantu was one of the provinces of Kenya, with the city of Kisumu as its capital.) This means that the ancient Hindus must have had some communication with the northern and southern ends of the Victoria Nyanza.

Cowrie shells from the Maldives were found in an Iron Age settlement near Nakuru, Kenya, which was found by Dr Mary Leakey. Indians who traded with Egypt used cowrie shells as money. This system dated as far back as the 28th century BCE. According to Arab geographers, the name Zangistan, from which the name Zanzibar or Zang Coast is derived, covers the whole of the eastern part of Africa. 'Zang' is the equivalent of the Sanskrit word '*sankh*'. The name Sankha Dvipa means the Island of Shells.

Golden Tara (Sailko, 2016). CC BY-SA 3.0.

The Great Philippines–India Connection

George Coedes (1886–1969), a French scholar of Southeast Asian archaeology and history, referred to India's influence on Thailand, Malaysia, Singapore, the Philippines, Cambodia and Vietnam as the 'Indianisation' of these countries. In this chapter, I am focusing on the Philippines.

The Philippines got its name from the Austrian prince who later became Prince Philip of Spain. The name was given by the Spanish explorer Jocano Lopez De Villalobos in 1544.

For at least two millennia before the arrival of the Spanish, the Philippines was ruled by Hindu and Buddhist kingdoms. Between the 9th and 14th centuries, the Javanese Buddhist king Sri Vijaya, who was also known as Rajanathe Vijaya, ruled the country, followed by the Hindu Majapahit kingdom. The influence of the empire of Srivijaya spread up to Madagascar around 1,200 years ago. A DNA study of the Malagasy people traced their origins to 30 founding mothers who sailed from Indonesia! The Malagasy language has many words of Sanskrit origin.

In around 1400, Sri Lumay founded the kingdom of Cebu and its surrounding 167 islands and islets. He was half Malay and half Tamil, and a prince of the famous Tamil Chola dynasty. The kingdom later passed on to Sri Humabon. Cebu is in the central region of the Philippines, and is around 560 kilometres from the present capital Manila.

Butuan, which is in Mindanao island in the southern Philippines, was a Hindu-Buddhist kingdom from 1091. It was known for its gold mines. The Spanish observed that gold the size of a walnut or an egg could be found by digging in the sand. The first king was Sri Bata Shaja. Among the other kings who followed was King Siagu. The last Hindu king, Tupas, was defeated by the Portuguese in 1565 and he converted to Christianity. Hindu kings Humabon and Silongan also converted to Christianity. The Spanish ruled the Philippines until 1898. They destroyed statues of the Hindu gods and embarked on a mission to Christianise the Philippines.

In 1971, a statue of a Hindu goddess was found on Mindanao island. Known as the Golden Tara, it is a 1.79kg, 21-carat-gold statue and is dated between the 13th and 14th centuries. In the Tabon Caves of the island of Palawan, there is a statue of Garuda. Garuda is the eagle carrier of Lord Vishnu. A copper statue of Lord Ganesha and a bronze alloy statue of Lord Shiva were found on Mactan Island, which is part of Cebu province.

Maharadia Lawana is a Maranao epic. The Maranao are the indigenous people living in the Lanao province of the island of Minadano. It is a predominantly Muslim area. Also known as the Lake people, they have a dance form called Singkil. The dance form is based on the epic of *Darangen*, which is an interpretation of the *Ramayana*. In Dr Juan Francisco's (1994) book *From Ayodhya to Pulu Agama Niog: Rama's Journey to the Philippines*, the author traces Lord Rama's journey into Southeast Asia. In 1993, the Philippines Education Theatre Association staged several performances of the Maranao version of the *Ramayana*. According to Francisco (1994), he had unearthed this version of the *Ramayana* 25 years earlier.

Mount Banahaw, the highest mountain in the Philippines, is considered sacred by the Filipino people. Annual pilgrimages are made to the sacred mountain by the majority Christian population of the country. This tradition is taken from the Hindu belief of worshipping mountains.

Pedro Chirino, a Spanish priest and historian, noted that many Filipino customs were of Indian origin, such as the mode of greeting, offering prayers before major construction work and the devotional area in the home (Churchill, 1977).

Francisco de Sande, the third Spanish governor and captain-general of the Philippines in 1577, referred to the country as Indian. He said 'The Indians of this country are not simple or foolish. Nor are they frightened by anything whatsoever. They can only be dealt with guns or gifts of gold and silver' (Blair and Robertson, 2004).

In 1989, what is known as the Laguna Copperplate Inscription was found near the Lumbang River. It is the earliest written document found in the Philippines, and it is dated around the ninth century. The inscription has many Sanskrit words as well as old Javanese and Malay words. According to Indologist Juan Francisco (Stuart, 2008), the inscription confirms links between the Tagales people of Philippines and the Srivijaya empire and the Hindu-Buddhist kingdoms of India.

According to Filipino anthropologist Felipe Landa Jocano (Stuart, 2008), Indian influence on Philippine society is seen in the syllabic writing. There are 336 words of Sanskrit origin, and 150 of them are identified as being the origins of some major Philippine terms. The Baybayin ancient script of the Philippines has its origins in the Indian Brahmi script. It has evolved into the modern Kulitan script of the Kapampangan language.

Tagalog, the first national language, was renamed Filipino. It has many words of Sanskrit origin. Some of them are as follows:

Tagalog	**Sanskrit**	**English**
Dalita	*Dharita*	One who suffers
Dukhna	*Dukha*	Poverty, unhappiness
Sampalataya	*Sampradaya*	Faith
Mukha	*Mukha*	Face
Tala	*Tara*	Star
Saksi	*Saksi*	Witness
Kalma	*Karma*	Fate
Damla	*Dharma*	Divine law
Lupa	*Rupă*	Face

Tagalog	Sanskrit	English
Sabla	*Sarva*	Every
Garula	*Garuda*	Eagle
Laksina	*Dakshin*	South (also a surname)
Laksamana	*Lakshmana*	Admiral (also a surname)
Kapas	*Kapas*	Cotton
Balita	*Varta*	News
Baya	*Bhayya*	Danger, fear
Gadya	*Gajah*	Elephant

The Present

Past president Ferdinand Marcos and the present (at time of writing) president, Rodrigo Duterte, both proposed that the name of the country should be changed to the Republic of Maharlika. This is based on the Sanskrit word *mahardhika*, meaning a man of wealth, knowledge and ability. During the brief British occupation of the Philippines, between 1762 and 1764, there was a mutiny by the Indian soldiers of the British Army. Many stayed on in the Philippines.

Over a million Filipinos are of full or partial Indian descent, as of 2020.

These are some famous Filipinos of Indian descent:

- Rabia Occena Mateo – Miss Universe Philippines in 2020.
- Ramon Bagatsing – The longest serving mayor of Manila, who served from 1971 to 1986. Ramon's father, Mataram Singh, was a Sikh. He was inspired by the Indian freedom fighter Bhagat Singh, and he opened a chapter of the revolutionary Ghadar Party in Manila. He later changed his name to Amado Bhagat Singh. Ramon was a war hero who fought for the Americans in the Second World War.
- Juan Cailles – An army commander who served during the Philippines Revolution and Philippine–American War.

Prambanan Temple, Yogyakarta, Indonesia (Cmichel67, 2016). CC BY-SA 4.0.

The Great Indonesia–India Connection

The first president of Indonesia, Suharto Sukarno (1946), wrote the following:

> *In the veins of every one of my people flows the blood of Indian ancestors and the culture that we possess is steeped through and through with Indian influences. Two thousand years ago people from your country came to Jawadvipa and Suvarnadvipa in the spirit of brotherly love. They gave the initiative to found powerful kingdoms such as those of Sri Vijaya, Mataram and Majapahit. We then learnt to worship the very gods that you now worship still and we fashioned a culture that even today is largely identical with your own. Later, we turned to Islam: but that religion too was brought by people coming from both sides of India.*

There are five main islands of Indonesia, namely Sumatra, Java, Kalimantan, Sulawesi and the Indonesian part of New Guinea (Papua New Guinea). The predominantly Hindu island of Bali is part of the lesser Sunda Islands.

The Hindu influence reached the Indonesian archipelago as early as the first century. By the fourth century, Hindu kingdoms had been established in the following areas: Kutai in East Kalimantan, Tarumanagara in West Java, and Holing (Kalingga) in Central Java. Kutai Martadipura was the first Hindu kingdom established in eastern Borneo. The seven stone pillars found in this area, dated at around 775 CE, attest to the Hindu presence. They were written in the Pallava language in the Sanskrit Devanagari script. The Pallava language originated in the place that is Tamil Nadu in the present day. It is named after the Pallava dynasty. It later evolved into the Balinese, Burmese, Khmer, Thai and Lao languages.

The Hindus brought with them art, culture, the rules of running a kingdom, town planning and expertise in many fields.

The Indonesian language Bahasa, which is actually a Sanskrit word meaning language, has thousands of Sanskrit-origin words.

The *Ramayana* and *Mahabharata* remain hugely popular in Indonesia even today. It is said that Sugriva, the commander of Lord Rama's army, sent some of his men to Java in search of Sita. These legends are shown in the Wayang puppet shows and dance performances. Wayang, which means shadow, is a puppet show whose origins are in 10th century southern India.

The Hindu king Sailendra converted to Mahayana Buddhism in around 800. He built the world's largest Buddhist temple, which is called Borobudur Temple. The temple complex is in Central Java, not far from the city of Yogyakarta.

The Day of Vesak (or Vaisakhi in Sanskrit) is the most sacred day to millions of Buddhists around the world. It was on the Day of Vesak two and a half millennia ago, in the year 623 BCE, that the Buddha was born. It was also on the Day of Vesak that the Buddha attained enlightenment, and it was on the Day of Vesak that the Buddha passed away in his eightieth year. The day falls on the day of the full moon around 13th April. In Indonesia, it is known as Hari Raya Waisak, and Buddhist monks, laymen and women make a pilgrimage to the Borobudur Temple that day.

The Sanjaya dynasty remained Hindu and built the magnificent Prambanan Temple in around 850. The temple is dedicated to the lords Brahma, Vishnu and Shiva. It too is in Central Java, not far from the Buddhist Borobudur Temple.

The temple was abandoned around 100 years after its construction. Over the years, the Dutch colonists and later the Indonesian government have done much to restore the temple.

Since 1960, a ballet of the *Ramayana* is performed every evening at the temple. According to Dore (2015), the *Ramayana* ballet was acknowledged by the Guinness Book as the most continuously staged performance in the world. Almost all the actors are Muslim, and they see no conflict of faith. According to them, the *Ramayana* and *Mahabharata* are part of their culture. Between 9th and 12th November 2019, the grand Abhiṣeka sacred ceremony was performed in this temple compound. This Hindu ritual was held here for the first time, 1,163 years after the Prambanan Temple was founded in 856. Indonesian Hindus believe that the Abhiṣeka ceremony has restored the sanctity of the temple.

King Kertanegara was the last king of the Singasari dynasty, which reigned from 1222 to 1292. He reconciled Hinduism and Buddhism. He recognised the oneness of Shiva and Buddha. The Majapahit dynasty began in 1293 and was at its peak between 1350 and 1389. The Majapahit dynasty is still a cause of great pride for Indonesians. The Majapahit empire stretched from Sumatra to New Guinea, and it consisted of present-day Indonesia, Singapore, Malaysia, Brunei, Southern Thailand, East Timor and parts of the Philippines. The Indonesian national motto – '*Bhinneka Tunggal Ika*', meaning 'Unity in Diversity' – originates from an old Javanese poem written during the rule of the Majapahit dynasty.

The End of the Hindu and Buddhist Empire of Indonesia

Sabdapalon was a priest and advisor to the last king of the Majapahit dynasty. The king's name was Brawijaya V. Against the advice of Sabdapalon, the king converted to Islam in 1478. This marked the end of the Hindu-Buddhist empire of Indonesia. In earlier times, whenever a king changed his religion, the subjects used to follow.

The Java Prophecies

The king's conversion caused Sabdapalon utter disappointment and anger. He cursed the king and said that the country would face huge calamities. He said he was leaving and would come back after 500 years, and the time of his return would be signalled by the eruption of Mount Merapi. He proclaimed that, on his return, the Hindu-Buddhist Javanese religion would be restored. He then disappeared, along with his fellow priest Nayagenggong. The 500 years were over in 2009, and although the prophecy has not come true, many Indonesians believe it will happen.

According to Ishak (2019), the Hindu Kediri dynasty ruled Java for 400 years. Between 1135 and 1179, it was ruled by a just and famous king called Jayabaya. His prophecies, which are known as *Serat Jayabaya*, mention that Java would be colonised by white people and they would be replaced by people from the north whose rule would not last long. Java would regain freedom after that. This prediction has proved correct. The Dutch were present in Java from 1600 and took full control from 1800. The Dutch had brought indentured labour from India, mainly from South India, but not exclusively. They were brought to work on tobacco plantations. They have now been in Indonesia for around four centuries and are completely integrated into Indonesian society.

During the Second World War, the Japanese pushed the Dutch out of Java in 1942. After their defeat in the Second World War, the Japanese handed the country over to the Indonesian people in 1945.

The final prophecy of King Jayabaya was that a just king would appear to bring a golden age to the country. This would happen at a time when carriages would be driven without horses, ships would fly through the sky, women would wear men's clothing, and children would neglect their parents!

Hindu Influence on Present-Day Indonesia

Hindu heritage remains very strong in the fabric of Indonesian society. The vehicle of Lord Vishnu, an eagle called Garuda, is the national emblem of Indonesia, and it is known as Garuda Pancasila. The Indonesian state stands on the idea of '*pancasila*', which is a Sanskrit word meaning five principles. The national airline is also called Garuda. The national currency is called the rupiah, which is from the same word origin as the Indian rupee. The 20,000-rupiah note has a picture of Lord Ganesha on it. The prestigious Bandung Institute of Technology has Lord Ganesha as its logo. The Indonesian military has Lord Hanuman as its mascot.

An Indonesian Navy admiral is called a Laksman, and the Air Chief Marshal is called Laksman Udara. Indonesians, irrespective of religion, have Hindu names such as Indra, Krishna, Surya, Rama and Sri.

According to McDaniel (2017), Hindu temples in Bali do a call to prayer that is similar to that of mosques; this is done twice a day, at 6am and 6pm. The prayers are called the Trisandhya and are played over loudspeakers. They start with the Gayatri Mantra.

Hinduism is also taught in schools, which does not happen even in India!

The island of Bali remains a majority Hindu island. According to the official statistics for 2010, there are around 4 million Hindus in Indonesia, though some believe there could be as many as 10 million.

At present, there are Hindu settlements around the Tengger mountain range as well as near Mount Bromo and the Mount Semeru volcano. The Tengger people form the biggest Hindu community in Java. They go on a pilgrimage to Mount Bromo every year, which is considered to be the abode of Lord Brahma. There is also a Hindu presence in Karanganyar Regency in Central Java and near Prambanan, as well as in the city of Yogyakarta. In the early 1970s, the Torajan people of Sulawesi, along with the Karo Batak people of Sumatra (in 1977) and the Ngaju Dayak people of Kalimantan (in 1980) converted to Hinduism. This form of Hinduism also includes the traditional animistic practices of these people. Over 100,000 people have converted to Hinduism in the last two decades.

The Osing people of East Java, numbering around 400,000, resisted conversion to Islam and remain Hindu. They too share their animist beliefs with their Hindu faith.

Some years ago, Happy Salma – who is an actress, model and writer – converted to Hinduism after marrying Balinese prince Tjokorda Bagus Dwi Santana Kerthyasa. In 2017, the Javan princess Kanjeng Raden Ayu Mahindrani Kooswidyanthi converted to Hinduism. Her conversion ceremony ended with the chanting of the Gayatri Mantra.

During Prime Minister Narendra Modi's visit to Indonesia in 2018, the Javan president Joko Jokowi informed Prime Minister Modi that his grandson was called Jan Ethes Srinarendra! In January 2020, President Joko Jokowi authorised the Hindu Dharma State Institute in Denpasar, Bali, to become the first Hindu university in the country. Many new temples have been built in recent times, and they are attracting more people to the Hindu faith.

There are around 250,000 people of Indian origin in Indonesia. They are mainly in the garment industry, information technology (IT), finance and engineering.

There are around 40 Indian associations, as well as temples and Sikh gurudwaras.

The ancient Hindus and modern day Hindus of Indonesia will cross paths, I am sure!

Scene from the *Ramakien* (Thai *Ramayana*) (Jpatokal, n.d.).
Public domain.

One of seven Vishnu statues in the Nat-Hlaung Kyaung temple, Bagan, Myanmar. Originally, there were 10 idols dedicated to Vishnu; three were removed, one of which is in the Berlin-Dahlem Museum (Hybernator, 2007). CC BY-SA 3.0.

The Great Thailand– and Myanmar–India Connections

The Hindu and Buddhist influence arrived in Thailand from 250 BCE onwards. Between the 9th and 13th centuries, Mahayana Buddhism flourished in Thailand. During the same time, the powerful Hindu Khmer Empire in Cambodia also had influence on Thailand. The old capital of Thailand was known as Ayutthaya, after Ayodhya, which is the capital city of Lord Rama's empire.

According to an article written by the Royal Thai Embassy (2018) in India:

> *The traditional names of many ruling Thai kings at least since the period of the Ayutthaya Kingdom (1351–1767) was either 'Ramesuan' or 'Ramathibodi' (Rama the Ruler)... Theoretically, the kings were considered to be the incarnation of the Hindu Lord Vishnu, as well as the Buddhist Bodhisattwa. The emblem of the Chakkri dynasty is Lord Vishnu's disc intersecting with Lord Shiva's Trishul or trident.*

All kings in the current Chakkri dynasty of Thailand are referred to as Rama. This tradition started in 1782.

This is said of King Rama I (1782–1809) (Royal Thai Embassy, 2018):

> *... with the help of Brahmins, scholars and poets, he translated and composed a completed Thai version of the* Ramayana *(called* 'Ramakian' *– or, 'the honour of Rama', in Thai) and built the Temple of Emerald Buddha in his grand palace. The*

walls of the temple compound are decorated in murals telling the story of Ramakian *in its entirety.*

King Vajiravudh, or Rama VI (1910–1925), was a scholar well versed in Sanskrit and Hindu literature, including the *Ramayana* and *Mahabharata*. He wrote plays based on Kalidasa's *Shakuntala* and King Harsha's *Priyadarshika*, the tales of King Nala and Princess Damayanti.

King Bhumibol Adulyadej, or Rama IX (1946–2016), was the patron of the first Thai Buddhist temple built in India at Bodh Gaya. This was as part of the celebrations in 1956 marking 2,500 years of Buddhism.

The current king, Maha Vajiralongkorn or Rama X, was crowned in 2019. His coronation was conducted by Brahmin priests who are well versed in Sanskrit and the Tamil language.

This link of the Buddhist kings of Thailand to South India's Chola dynasty goes back to the 11th century.

Modern Hindu Icons in Thailand

Thailand's international airport in Bangkok is called Suvarnabhumi, which is a word of Sanskrit origin, meaning the golden land. It has a huge mural showing the churning of the ocean, which is a famous Hindu legend. This legend is very famous with the people of Thailand. The airport also has a huge golden statue of Ravana.

Images of Lord Ganesha, who is known in Thailand as Phra Pikanet, can also be seen all over Thailand. Lord Ganesha is worshipped before any venture is started, just as in India. Three giant statues of Lord Ganesha can be found in Thailand's Chachoengsao Province. The first statue, which is of a seated Ganesha, is at Wat Phrong Akat; the second is a standing statue at Khlong Kuean Ganesh International Park; and the third, a reclining one, is at Wat Saman Rattanaram. This area could be visited on a day trip from Bangkok.

Lords Brahma, Vishnu and Shiva are also revered in Thailand. Lord Hanuman is considered to be the patron of martial arts, as an example of courage, fortitude and excellence. Muay Thai, a 4,000-year-old martial arts discipline, is also known as Hanuman Thai Boxing.

There is a Hindu temple that was established in 1784 by King Rama I. It is called Devasthan and is in the Phra Nakhon District of Bangkok. It is also home to the descendants of priests who arrived there around 1,000 years ago. Phimai Historical Park near Phimai in the Nakhon Ratchasima Province of Thailand is a massive Buddhist temple that was built by the Hindu Khmer rulers in nearby Cambodia. In size, it is as big as the Angkor Wat Hindu temple of Cambodia. The temple depicts many Hindu deities. It signifies the acceptance and tolerance of the two major religions with roots in India.

The Myanmar–India Connection

The country of Myanmar, which used to be called Burma, was known as Brahma Desa. Myanmar is the regional language transliteration of Brahma. Under British rule, Myanmar was part of India until 1937.

According to the Royal Historical Commission of Burma (1829–1832), King Abhi Raja from India established a kingdom in 850 BCE. His son also established a kingdom in the Arakan region of Myanmar, which is the lower coastal area of the country. The kings of this dynasty, of which there were 31, continued their rule of this region.

It was the Mon people from China who first brought Buddhism to Myanmar. The Mon people were heavily influenced by Hindu culture and Emperor Ashoka's Buddhist kingdom of India. The Mon kingdom was originally known as Ramandesa, but later became known as Dvaravati, meaning city of gates. They ruled between the 6th and 11th centuries.

Dhammasattha is the Buddhist law written in the Pali and Sanskrit languages that formed the legal structure of Burma from 1250 to 1850. It is still used in the courts today on family and inheritance matters. Both Pali and Sanskrit were court languages during this time.

Yamanyana, the Buddhist version of the *Ramayana*, is hugely popular in Myanmar. *Yama Zat Pwe* stage shows (dramatic performances of the Rama story) are still held regularly. From the reign of King Anawrahta (1044-77) of the Pagan region, now known as Bagan, which is located on the eastern bank of Irrawaddy River, the *Ramayana* epic was passed on orally from generation to generation. In 1775, U Aung Phyo wrote down the Myanmar version of the *Ramayana*, called *Rama Thagyin*, meaning *Song from Ramayana*. According to Gallop (2014), the *Ramayana* came to be regarded in the 18th century as a noble saga even by Buddhist monks. In the 19th century, at the height of its popularity, the *Ramayana* was performed in the royal palace by royal troupes and professional artists.

According to Leider (2006), Brahmins, known as Punna, played an important role in Burma. In the royal court, they performed the ceremony of installing a new king. One core element of the ritual was to pour water from a conch on the head of the king-to-be. The Brahmins also presided over weddings, ear piercing, the first feeding of rice to a baby, and other ceremonies. Lord Ganesha (known as Maha Peinnay), Lord Shiva (known as Parmeshwar), his wife (known as Chandi), Kali, Parvati and Uma were also worshipped.

Thingyan, the annual Myanmar festival, stems from a Buddhist version of a Hindu legend of Lord Brahma. It mostly takes place between 13th and 16th April every year. It is a festival of great merriment. People splash water over each other, just like the Hindu festival of Holi. Fish from dry rivers or lakes are collected and released into bigger lakes as an act of good karma.

Buddhism in Present-Day Myanmar

The Buddhist practice of merit is about abstaining from killing, stealing, lying, adultery and alcohol. Many prominent Buddhist monks have promoted vegetarianism, including Thamanya Sayadaw (1910–2003) and Mahasi Sayadaw (1904–1982), who introduced Vipassana meditation to the West.

The Indian Presence in Myanmar Today

Under the British Raj, there were almost 1 million Indians in the country by 1931, mostly from Tamil Nadu and Bengal. By 1942, almost half the population of Rangoon (now known as Yangon) was Indian. Around 500,000 left after the Japanese invasion of 1942. In 1964, 300,000 were expelled by General Ne Win.

However, the Indian community continues to wield considerable influence and control over the Myanmar economy. Satya Narayan Goenka (1924–2013) was born in Myanmar and became a prominent teacher of Vipassana meditation.

Benzaiten (Fabio from Rome, Italy, 2008). CC BY-SA 2.0.

The Great Japan–India Connection

Yasukuni Enoki, Ambassador of Japan to India (2004 to 2007), said 'It is very important for the Japanese to know that in the bottom of Japanese culture, Indian culture is very firmly imprinted.' Furthermore, he also stated this (Indian Diplomacy, 2015):

> *There are hundreds of shrines to Goddess Saraswati and innumerable representations of Lakshmi, Indra, Shiva, Brahma, Mahakala, Ganesha, Agni, Bhudevi, Garuda, Kamadeva, Yama, and other deities. In a sense Japan is a time capsule of Hindu culture that disappeared in India. In fact, deities that have practically been forgotten in India, such as Vayu and Varuna, are still worshipped in Japan. The most ancient temple to Lord Ganesha, which has been in use for more than a thousand years, is located in Tokyo. The Hindu ritual of a* 'homa' *or* 'havan' *(*'goma' *in Japanese) is performed with the same regularity in Japan as in India. A* havan *is a ritual conducted during the worship of the Fire/Agni, and it is performed with the same mantras and with the utterance of the word* 'Swa-ha' *– which should make an Indian feel right at home in a Japanese Temple!*

(The prayers and mantras recited are in Sanskrit in the Siddha script, which was prevalent around the fifth century. The Siddha script has long been replaced in India with the Devanagari script, but it continues to be used in Japan).

The Goddess of Laxmi Town

A town near Tokyo, Japan – Kichijōji – has been named after the Hindu goddess Lakshmi. According to Kitagawa (2018), Consul General of Japan in India, 'You will be surprised to know that the town near Tokyo has its origin from Lakshmi temple. Kichijōji means Lakshmi temple in Japanese.' Commenting upon the influence India had on the Japanese culture and society, Kitagawa also concluded that 'many might think Japan and India are different, though they are not'.

The influence of Hinduism on Japan is noted in an article written by Professor Nakamura (1912–1999) for *Japan Times* (Nakamura, 1992):

> *Although Japan is far from India geographically, the two countries have close cultural relations and contacts in other areas. Cultural relations between the two can be traced back to very early times. Without Indian influence, Japanese culture would not be what it is today. As most Japanese profess the Buddhist faith, they have generally been influenced by Indian ideas.*

In the same article, Nakamura (1992) goes on to describe the initial spread of Buddhism in Japan:

> *The new religion began to be widely professed, partly due to the arrival in Japan of missionaries, magicians, the scriptures, and various accessories for rituals, etc. Buddhism received its first imperial patronage from Prince Shotoku (574–621), who became regent to the Lady Emperor Suiko in 593. He drew up Japan's first Constitution, proclaiming the 'Three Treasures' (triratna), i.e. The Buddha, The Dharma (doctrine) and The Sangha (the Order), to be the ultimate objects of faith, and single-minded devotion to them to be the fundamental factor of an upright life.*
>
> *At government expense, he built Buddhist temples, pagodas, seminaries, hospitals, dispensaries and asylums for the aged and*

> *the destitute. Horyuji Temple, built by him near the city of Nara, the then capital of Japan, is the oldest wooden building in the world.*
>
> *Under his reign (593–621) the Japanese came into direct contact with Chinese Buddhism. He sent students to China to study Buddhist doctrines. From his time onwards, the influence of Buddhism continued to be conspicuous almost without interruption to the close of the Tokugawa regime (1868).*

Furthermore, Nakamura (1992) also explains who is believed to have been the first Indian to visit Japan and his influence on that country:

> *Over the past 1,200 years, Indians have visited Japan from time to time. Probably the first Indian to come to our land was Bodhisena, a Buddhist monk. He was born of a Brahmin family in India. His clan* (gotra) *was Bharadvaja.* [He was from Tamil Nadu, either from the city of Madurai or Kanchipuram.]
>
> *Receiving a mystic inspiration from Manjushri Bodhisattva, he went to China and lived in the Wu T'ai Shan Mountain.* ['Bodhisattva' means one who is the Buddha to be and has supreme knowledge. 'Manjushri' means gentle or sweet glory. There was a Manjushri Pala dynasty in India in the ninth century. Bodhisattva, who is also known as Bodhisena and Bodhidharma, started Chan Buddhism in China, which is known in Japan as Zen Buddhism.]
>
> *At the request of several Japanese who were in China for diplomatic negotiations and to study, Bodhisena came to Japan along with other Buddhist monks from China and Indo-China in 736. He was cordially received by the Imperial family, and was appointed archbishop. People informally called him Baramon (Brahmana) archbishop.* [He is also known in Japan as Daruma, which comes from the Sanskrit word '*dharma*'.] *He always recited the Buddha Avatamsaka-sutra, and was versed in magical formulae.*

Bodhisena in Japan

According to Pallavi Aiyar (2018), the Indian monk Bodhisena, founder of the Kegon school of Buddhism, died in 760 and is buried in Ryusenji Temple on the slopes of Mount Omine. Unlike some historical Buddhist sects, the Kegon school continues to flourish today, with its headquarters at Nara's Tōdai-ji temple, which is a United Nations Educational, Scientific and Cultural Organization (UNESCO) World Heritage site. Founded in 738 and officially opened in 752, Tōdai-ji is best known for its 500-tonne, 15-metre-high Buddha, which is the largest bronze statue in the world.

This gargantuan sculpture, known as the *Daibutsu*, was commissioned by the Emperor Shomu in the year 743 in the hope of gaining divine favour and thereby reversing the effects of a devastating drought, compounded by an outbreak of smallpox that had ravaged the area in 737.

The hall that houses the *Daibutsu* is one of the world's largest wooden structures. It is Nara's most popular tourist destination and is thronged with visitors from around the world. After gawping at the *Daibutsu*, they usually head to a hole in one of the pillars that holds up the edifice. According to legend, the hole is the exact size of one of the Buddha statue's nostrils, and anyone who crawls through it will gain enlightenment, albeit in their next life. No one seems to know the exact dimensions of the hole/nostril, but it is large enough for a child to tunnel through with relative ease.

Of all the eminent Buddhist scholars in Nara at the time, it was Bodhisena who was chosen to perform the statue's 'eye opening' ceremony. In front of a huge, cosmopolitan gathering that included ambassadors from Persia, Korea, Vietnam, China and Central Asia, Bodhisena painted the pupils on the eyes of the Buddha statue, inviting the spirit in to animate the sculpture.

Vegetarianism in Japan

Both Japan's national religions of Buddhism and Shintoism promote plant-based eating. In 676, the then Japanese emperor Tenmu proclaimed an ordinance prohibiting the eating of fish and shellfish as well as animal flesh and fowl. Subsequently, in the year 737 of the Nara period, Emperor Shomu approved of the eating of fish and shellfish. During the 1,200 years from the Nara period to the Meiji restoration in the latter half of the 19th century Japan was practically vegetarian. In seventh-century Japan, the Empress Jito encouraged '*hojoe*', or the releasing of captive animals, and established wildlife preserves where animals could not be hunted. *Hojoe* is a religious ritual in which captive animals are released into the wild to admonish against the taking of life. Buddhism is based on the precept that the taking of life is forbidden, and this was adopted by the Shinto faith as a result of the overlap of Shintoism and Buddhism in Japan. The ritual encompasses harvest festivals and thanksgiving festivals, and it is conducted in spring and autumn in Buddhist temples and Hachiman Shin temples throughout Japan. (Hachiman is the ancient Shinto god or *kami* of war, divination and culture).

Further Observations

Apart from Japan, the following Buddhist countries have also been deeply influenced by India: China, Thailand, Cambodia, Myanmar, Bhutan, Sri Lanka, Tibet, Laos, Vietnam, Macau and Taiwan.

Philip Rawson (1967) declared this:

> *'The culture of India has been one of the world's most powerful civilizing forces. Countries of the Far East, including China, Korea, Japan, Tibet and Mongolia owe much of what is best in their own cultures to the inspiration of ideas imported from India. The West, too, has its own debts. But the members of that circle of civilisations beyond Burma* [Myanmar] *scattered around the Gulf of Siam and the Java Sea virtually owe their existence to the creative influence of Indian ideas… No conquest or invasion, no forced conversion. They were adopted because the people saw they were good and they could use them… their code of living, their conceptions of law and kingship, their rich literature and highly evolved philosophy of life.*

Hu Shih (1891–1962) was one of the most significant philosophers and intellectuals of China during the early 20th century. He was a professor of philosophy at Peking University as well as the Chinese ambassador to the US. He said 'India conquered and dominated China culturally for 20 centuries without ever having to send a soldier across the border.'

Panorama of giant Buddhist sculptures in a section of the Longmen Grottoes, including statues of Vairocana, Kasyapa, Ananda, Guanyin, Mahasthamaprapta and the Four Heavenly Kings. It dates mostly from the Northern Wei (386–534) and Tang dynasties (618–907) (WikiLaurent, 2010). CC BY-SA 3.0.

A Buddhist *stupa* in the collection of the Palace Museum, Beijing (Chez Casver, 2008). CC BY-SA 2.0.

The Great China–India Connection

The word 'China' originates from the Sanskrit word '*Cina*'. This is confirmed by many sources, including Arnold Hermann Ludwig Heeren (1760–1842). There are records of a China–India connection as far back as 5,000 years. In the great war of the *Mahabharata*, there is mention of Chinese soldiers. Tamil traders were present in Quezon and Fujian provinces in medieval times.

Hu Shih (1891–1962), a former Chinese ambassador to the US, said 'India conquered and dominated China culturally for 20 centuries without ever having to send a soldier across her border.'

Lin Yutang (1895–1976), author of *The Wisdom of India*, stated 'Not until we see the richness of the Hindu mind and its essential spirituality can we understand India. India was China's teacher in religion and imaginative literature, and the world's teacher in trigonometry, quadratic equations, grammar, phonetics, Arabian nights, animal fables, chess as well as philosophy and she inspired Boccaccio, Goethe, Herder, Schopenhauer and Emerson.'

The following interesting connections of China to India have been identified by Nayyar (2017):

- Buddhism was introduced to China by Han Emperor Ming-Ti or Mingdi (57/58–75/76). The emperor dreamt of a golden flying deity, which he believed to be Buddha Shakyamuni. He dispatched emissaries to India, who returned with *The Sutras of Forty-Two Sections*. These are quotes of the Lord Buddha. Two Indian monks –

Dharmaratna and Kasyapa Matanga – came to China and translated Buddhist tracts into Chinese. Another monk by the name of Parmartha arrived in China in 546 and spent 12 years in the area now called Guangzhou. He introduced Mahayana Buddhism. Buddhist monks from Kashmir went to China in large numbers in the fifth and sixth centuries.

- Chinese monks also travelled to India. A monk by the name of Fa Hien went to India in 399. He visited what is now Patna, learnt Sanskrit, copied the Vinaya rules and introduced them to China. The Vinaya rules is a set of disciplinary rules that the Buddhist monks and nuns have to follow.
- Under the Tang dynasty (618–907) Indian and Buddhist influence grew in China. Chinese students came in large numbers to the famous Buddhist university of Nalanda, which flourished in the sixth and seventh centuries under the Gupta Empire and later under Harsha, the emperor of Kannauj (located in what is the present-day state of Uttar Pradesh). Based near the city of Patna in the Indian state of Bihar, the university thrived for 700 years; at its peak, it had 10,000 students and monks from countries as far away as Greece and Persia. It had 2,000 teachers. Among the subjects on offer were Buddhism, Brahmanical philosophy, maths, astronomy and medicine. It had the world's biggest library.
- The most famous Chinese monk to visit India was Hiuen Tsang. He went to India in 630 and returned to China in 645. On his return, he was given a royal welcome, which speaks volumes about the veneration that the Chinese had for Buddhism and Indian culture. His book *Si-Yu-Ki* gave a strong impetus to the love of Indian culture in China.
- Another famous monk, I-tsing or Yijing, spent 10 years at Nalanda and returned to China with 4,000 Sanskrit manuscripts containing more than 50,000 *slokas* or hymns.

> He also compiled a Sanskrit-Chinese dictionary. Yijing also translated hymns from *Harivansh* (detailing the lineage of Hari or Lord Krishna) as an appendix to the epic *Mahabharata*.

According to Acharya (2021), a monk named Xuanzang said that Lord Buddha was bright like the moon and India was its source. Xuanzang travelled to India as a pilgrim in the seventh century and visited Nalanda University. He was honoured by King Harsha. The honour of being the most popular figure in Chinese Buddhism goes to Bodhisattva Guanyin (the one who perceives the laments of the world). He was an Indian monk whom the Chinese believed to be a superior being who helps those suffering in the world. Also known as Bodhidharma and as Damo all over China, he was established to be a prince from South India. Images of Damo can be found all over China. He is regarded as the first patriarch of Chan Buddhism, which is also known as Zen Buddhism in Japan.

According to Deepak (2020), a dictionary of Buddhism compiled by Japanese scholars lists more than 35,000 entries of Sanskrit words in the Chinese language. The Indian styles of painting and music, as well as medicine and astronomy were highly prized in China. Apart from translations of Buddhist scriptures, Chinese texts from the 2nd to the 12th century suggest that some 150 scholars focused on translating Hindu Sanskrit texts such as the *Vedas*, which are referred to as *Ming-Lun* (the science of knowledge) or *Zhi-Lun* (the science of intelligence).

In the 12th century, Nalanda University was burnt to the ground by Bakhtiar Khalji. He was a Turko-Afghan military general who had conquered parts of East India and Bihar. It could be argued that it was the biggest act of vandalism, and it destroyed the accumulated knowledge of thousands of years and reversed human progress for a long time.

When translating *Tao Te Chang*, which is the classic Chinese text written by sage Lieh Tzu (the founder of Taoism) in the sixth century, Arthur Waley (1889–1996), an orientalist and Sinologist, observed this:

> *I see no reason to doubt, that the 'holy mountain-men'* (sheng-hsien) *described by Lieh Tzu are Indian Rishi; and when we read in* Chuang Tzu *of certain Taoists who practiced movements very similar to the Asanas of Hindu yoga, it is at least a possibility that some knowledge of the yoga technique which these Rishi used had also drifted into China.*

Many Chinese believed that Lieh Tzu was reborn as Lord Buddha. Both Lieh Tzu and Lord Buddha were worshipped at the same altar. Taoism, which is also known as Daoism, is a religion that began in the sixth century. Buddhism and Taoism complement each other, sharing many beliefs. Emperor Ashoka of India (273–232 BCE) sanctioned the building of 84,000 *stupas*, out of which around 19 were in China. Some of Lord Buddha's ashes were distributed to each one of them.

From China, Buddhism went to Korea in the fourth century CE, and from there it extended to Japan in the sixth century.

Present-day China is officially an atheist state, which it has been since the Cultural Revolution that started in 1966. Buddhists faced massive persecution, and in Beijing alone, thousands of Buddhist cultural relics were destroyed. Buddhist monks were tortured, and sacred books were burnt. However, there is a huge revival of Buddhism in China at present. There are currently 245 million Buddhists in China and more than this number follow Buddhist beliefs along with other traditional beliefs. Buddhist monks and nuns are strict vegetarians, and they inspire other followers to become vegetarian.

Eight-armed Vishnu statue, Angkor Wat, Cambodia (Sebastian, 2009).

The 10th-centuary Trà Kiệu pedestal supports a massive lingam and ablutionary cistern (DoktorMax, 2007).

The Great Cambodia–Vietnam– and Laos–India Connections

Cambodia

In the Khmer language of Vietnam, the name Cambodia is Kampuchea, which is derived from the Sanskrit name Kambujadesa. Known first as the kingdom of Funan, it was founded in the first century and flourished for some 500 years. The Funan kingdom was succeeded by the Hindu Khmer state of Chenla, which existed till the ninth century.

The Hindu and Buddhist influence came to Cambodia from Hindu merchants. From the second century, Hinduism became the state religion of the Khmer people. The Khmer kings practised statecraft, art and sciences, plus they built extensive canal systems based on Indian expertise.

After that, a king named Jayavarman II (who ruled from about 800–850) established a capital at Angkor in central Cambodia. The empire flourished from the 9th to the 13th century under Jayavarman VII. He built the great temple of Angkor Wat in the 12th century. It is the largest temple complex in the world.

There was a shift away from Hinduism to Buddhism by the beginning of the 13th century, King Jayavarman VII took part in a Burmese (Myanmar) led mission to Sri Lanka to study the Theravada Buddhist canon in the Pali language. The king also sent his son

Tamilinda to Sri Lanka to be ordained as a Buddhist monk and to study Theravada Buddhism. He studied at the famous Mahavihara monastery in Sri Lanka. Theravada monks brought about a social and cultural revolution. The monasteries became a source of learning.

By the 19th century, the literacy rate in Cambodia was higher than that of Europe. Hinduism and Buddhism coexisted peacefully at that time. The royal palace in Phnom Penh houses a sword that is said to have been given by the god Indira himself.

Reamker or *Ramakerti*, which means the *Glory of Rama*, is the national epic of Cambodia. According to '*Reamker*' (2021), this adapted version of the *Ramayana* is an integral part of Cambodian culture. It is the mainstay of the Royal Ballet's repertoire. It is performed in a Khmer dance theatre called L'Khaon. The walls of the famous Angkor Wat temple complex depict scenes from the *Ramayana* dating back nearly a millennium.

According to Woźnica (2010), the Khmer script has descended from the Indian Brahmi script, and the Khmer language has borrowed heavily from Sanskrit and the Pali language.

Almost 97 per cent of Cambodians remain Buddhist to this day.

Vietnam

In what is now the central and southern part of Vietnam, the Hindu kingdom of Champa was established around the fourth century.

According to Parker (2015), the first Champa king was a Tamil by the name Sri Maran. The Champa kingdom was divided into five regions, which are named after regions in India. They were Indrapura (present-day Dong Duong), Amravati (present-day Quang Nam), Vijaya (present-day Binh Dinh), Kauthara (present-day Nha Trang) and Panduranga (present-day Phan Rang). In the Quang Nam area, there are many ruined Hindu temples dedicated to Lord Shiva. In 400 CE, Champa was united under the rule of King Bhadravarman.

After decades of battles with invading neighbours and counter invasions, in the 17th century the Champa kingdom was absorbed into what is today Vietnam. There are 60,000 Cham Hindus in Vietnam at present. They have kept alive their ancient heritage.

According to Parker (2015), the site of the ancient Son Tien Tu Pagoda on top of Mount Ba is considered the most spiritual and sacred place in Vietnam. There, on a three-metre-high granite rock, is the Ban Chan Tien, a huge footprint belonging to a god, who set his footprint there at the dawn of humankind. The fifth Quang Nam Heritage festival held in 2013 displayed a 3,500- to 4,000-year-old Lord Vishnu sculpture. That makes it the oldest Hindu artefact found anywhere in the world. Other artefacts that have been found in Vietnam are 320 gold plaques decorated with Garuda, the eagle carrier of Lord Vishnu; Lord Narasimha; Lord Kurma; and the goddess Durga.

The name of the famous Mekong River that flows through Vietnam and many other countries is derived from Mae Nam Khong. The word '*Khong*' is Sanskrit for the Ganges. It is generally just called the River Khong.

Buddhism came to Vietnam in the second or third century. During the Dinh dynasty (968–980), Buddhism was recognised as a state religion. Buddhism reached its zenith during the Ly dynasty, whose founder was Ly Thai.

In 1887, the French colonised Vietnam and called it French Indochina. Catholic missionaries from Spain and Portugal had been to Vietnam in the 16th century on evangelism missions. They were followed by Jesuits from Italy, Portugal and Japan. French missionaries of the Foreign Missions Society and Spanish missionaries of the Dominican Order also came to Vietnam.

In 1954, Vietnam was divided into two countries by the French. The north part was led by communist revolutionary Ho Chi Minh. While the north was supported by China, the non-communist south was supported by the French and the US. From 2nd March 1965 to 2nd November 1968, the US carpet bombed North Vietnam. The US eventually lost its battle against the communist guerrillas, and the country was reunited in 1970. Saigon, the capital of South

Vietnam was renamed Ho Chi Minh City. Ho Chi Minh once said 'I and others may be revolutionaries but we are disciples of Mahatma Gandhi directly or indirectly. Nothing more, nothing less. Buddhism remains the largest religion in Vietnam.'

Laos

Theravada Buddhism came to Laos during the seventh and eighth centuries. It came from the ancient kingdom of Dvaravati, which was ruled by the Mon people based in Thailand. Around 65 per cent of the population is Buddhist at the time of writing.

The Lao script is derived from the Sanskrit and Pali languages. The Laotian *Ramayana*, which is called *Phra Lak Phra Ram*, forms an important part of the culture of the country. The Lao *Ramayana* interprets Lord Rama as the incarnation of Buddha rather than Vishnu, as in the Indian *Ramayana*. According to Lonely Tours (n.d.), for almost 15 centuries, the *Ramayana* was performed by the Royal Ballet troupe. In 1975, the *Ramayana* performance was banned. In 2002, the Royal Ballet troupe was revived and it now performs three times a week at the Royal Palace in Luang Prabang, and it also undertakes foreign tours.

Queen Heo-Hwang-Ok's memorial on the west bank of the Saryu River, Ayodhya, India. (Rémi Cormier, 2007).

The Great Korea–, Tibet–, Mongolia– and Bhutan– India Connection

Korea

According to Professor Kim Do-Young (Mandhani, 2018), a Delhi-based expert on Korean studies, there is an 'ancient bond' between the two nations of India and South Korea.

This article by Nikita Mandhani (2018) explains that Ayodhya – the birth place of Lord Rama in India – has a special significance for South Koreans. They believe that an Indian princess, Suriratna from Ayodhya (who is also known as Heo Hwang-ok), travelled to Korea and married King Kim Suro. She went there in 48 CE – some 2,000 years ago. They had 10 sons, and their dynasty is known as the Karak dynasty. The descendants of the couple number more than 6 million at time of writing – almost 10% of the population of South Korea. Buddhism arrived in the Korean Peninsula from China in the fourth century. It remains a Buddhist country. Although North Korea is officially atheist, Buddhism influences its customs and traditions.

In 2000, an agreement was signed to twin the cities of Ayodhya and Gimhae, South Korea. In 2001, more than 100 historians and government officials unveiled Queen Heo Hwang-ok's memorial on the west bank of the Saryu River in Ayodhya. On her visit to Ayodhya in November 2018, the first lady of South Korea, Kim Jung-Sook, attended a ceremony to mark the commencement of the monument's upgrade. In 2019, South Korea and India signed an agreement to release a joint stamp commemorating Queen Heo Hwang-ok.

Tibet

Buddhism came to Tibet from India in the seventh century. A Tibetan king, Tri Songdetsen, invited two Buddhist masters from India to visit. The first was Shantarakshita, followed by Padmasambhava, who was a Tantric '*mahasiddha*' (a master of miraculous powers). Also known as Guru Rinpoche, Padmasambhava was a legendary Indian monk who established the first Buddhist monastery in Tibet in 749 CE.

Between the 11th and 12th centuries, Tibetans travelled to India to acquire and translate Buddhist texts with the assistance of renowned Indian master Atisa, who had arrived in Tibet in 1042.

In 1951, communist China annexed Tibet, and in 1959, the Tibetan spiritual leader – the Dalai Lama – fled to India. The Dalai Lama and around 100,000 Tibetans live in Dharamshala, which is in the Indian state of Madhya Pradesh. They long to go back to Tibet as free people to keep their Buddhist faith and culture alive.

Mongolia

Many people think that the Mongolians were originally the Mughals who plundered India and committed genocidal atrocities. The Mughals were mostly ethnically Turks, with some from other tribes, though some of them claimed distant Mongol connections. However, the 13th-century emperor Genghis Khan actually practiced shamanism, which involves linking to the spirit world. He was tolerant of all faiths.

His son Kubla Khan, the founder of the Yuan dynasty (1271–1368) became a Buddhist. According to the 2020 census (Office of International Religious Freedom, 2021b), 87.1% of the Mongolian population is Buddhist.

Bhutan

Buddhism was first introduced to Bhutan from Tibet in the 8th-century by an Indian Tantric *mahasiddha*. The third king of Bhutan, Jigme Dorji Wangchuck (1952–1972), was a visionary also known as the 'father of modern Bhutan'. According to the Khyentse Foundation (2015), he commissioned the manufacture of 10,000 gilded bronze images of the Buddha, and he oversaw the publication of astounding editions of the 108-volume *Kanjur* (*Translation of the Word [of the Buddha]*) and the 225-volume *Tenjur* (*Translation of Teachings [on Buddhism]*), as well as the construction of numerous chorten (*stupas*) throughout the country. Around 83% of Bhutan's population was Buddhist according to the 2020 census (Office of International Religious Freedom, 2021a).

'*Lokapalas*' is a Sanskrit word meaning guardians and protectors. Common to both Hinduism and Buddhism is the idea of four protectors, one for each of four directions (north, south, east and west).

Pompeii Lakshmi is an ivory statue that was discovered in the ruins of Pompeii, Italy. The statue dates from the first century CE. It may also be a representative of a *Yaksi* – a god of fertility. The statue is now housed in the Secret Museum in the Naples National Archaeological Museum (Sailko, 2013). CC BY-SA 3.0.

Karyasiddhi Hanuman statue at the Dattatreya Mandir in Orange Field Village, Carapichaima, Caroni County, Couva-Tabaquite Talparo, Trinidad and Tobago (Grueslayer, 2016). CC BY-SA 4.0.

India's Influence and Presence in Other Countries

In the 19th century, the colonial powers brought tens of thousands of Indians as indentured labour to work on tobacco, cotton and sugarcane plantations in their colonies. They were also known as Girmityas, which is the Indian pronunciation of the word meaning agreement, which refers to the agreement they signed with the British colonial power. They were also known as Jahajis, which means those who went by ship.

Italy

The Pompeii Lakshmi statue shown in the first photo on the previous page is more proof of ancient Indian influence, but this time in Italy.

Mauritius

Beginning in 1836, tens of thousands of Indians came to Mauritius as indentured labour to work on sugar plantations. At the time of writing, 75 per cent of the population of Mauritius is of Indian origin, and Hinduism is the biggest religion. India is building strong ties with the country, and the head of the Mauritius naval forces and Mauritius national security advisors are Indian officers.

Seychelles

Hinduism is the second largest religion throughout the islands, and Hindus constitute 2.4 per cent of the population. The present president of the Seychelles, at the time of writing, is Wavel Ramkalawan. His great grandfather left for Mauritius in 1883. The family later moved to the Seychelles. The president has traced his roots to the Indian state of Bihar. India is building strong ties with this country.

Trinidad and Tobago

According to the 2011 census, there were over 240,000 Hindus in the country at that time and Hinduism is the second largest religion.

Basdeo Panday was the first prime minister of Trinidad and Tobago, serving between 1995 and 2001.

Kamla Persad Bissessar was the first woman and Hindu to become prime minister of the country, serving between 2010 and 2015. Her great-great-grandfather Ram Lakhan Mishra left for Trinidad and Tobago on 18th July 1889 from the village of Bhelpur in Bihar. In 2012, Kamla made a visit to her ancestral village of Bhelpur and was overcome with emotion. The villagers received her as a long-lost relative. She ended her welcome speech with '*Jai* Bihar, *Jai* Hind and *Jai* Trinidad' (where '*jai*' means victory).

Fiji

Brought to Fiji as indentured labour by the British, Hindus make up 40 per cent of the population, at the time of writing.

Mahendra Choudhry was the prime minister of Fiji between 1999 and 2000. He traced his ancestry to the village of Bahu Jamalpur in the Rohtak district of Haryana.

The Indian Space Research Organisation has a satellite tracking and intelligence station in Fiji.

Hindi is the official language of Fiji. The dialects spoken in Fiji, Suriname, Guyana, and Trinidad and Tobago are Bhojpuri and Awadhi, which originate from the Bihar state of India.

Suriname

Almost 38 per cent of Suriname's population is of Indian origin at the time of writing. Ashwin Adhin, who is of Indian origin, was the youngest vice president of Suriname from 2015–2020. Aashna Kanhai, who is the Surinamese ambassador to India, is also of Indian origin.

Guyana

Those Guyanese who are of Indian origin comprise the largest ethnic group in the country. There are around 270,000 Hindus in the country, at the time of writing. The presidents of the country who were/are of Indian origin have been Cheddi Jagan, Bharrat Jagdeo and Donald Ramotar.

The Hindu epic the *Ramayana* is very popular in Guyana as well as in Trinidad and Tobago, Suriname, and Fiji. Known as *Ramcharitmanas* in Guyana and composed by 16th-century poet-saint Tulsidas, it is the main text of Hinduism in these countries. It is said that, after working on the plantations during the day, the Indian labourers used to recite the *Ramayana* in the evenings. It was a great source of comfort to their otherwise very difficult lives.

Madagascar

There are 25,000 people of Indian origin in Madagascar, at the time of writing. Indians came to Madagascar around 150 years ago. There is, however, a far older connection with India. DNA evidence suggests that the Malagasy people can trace their genetic heritage to 30 different mothers from Indonesia around 1,200 years ago. At the time, Indonesia was under the Hindu Majapahit empire.

There are many Sanskrit loan words in the Malagasy language.

In 2013, scientists discovered that Madagascar and India were part of a single continent 85 million years ago!

Other Countries

Other countries where Indians have a large presence and substantial economic hold are Kenya, Uganda, Tanzania and South Africa.

Over the last 50 years, the Indian migration to the US, UK, Australia and Canada has created a strong foothold in these countries. People of Indian origin are holding powerful political positions and are high achievers in these countries, on both economic and academic grounds.

In the years to come, there could be a big Indian diaspora to the Eastern European countries and South American countries.

Tributes to India from Some of the Great Thinkers and Philosophers

Many great thinkers and philosophers have paid glowing tributes to India's contribution to the world over the ages. This chapter covers a selection of these.

Syrian astronomer Severus Sebokht (662) said 'I shall not now speak of the knowledge of Hindus… of their subtle discoveries in the science of astronomy, discoveries even more ingenious than those of Greeks and Babylonians. Their valuable method of calculation and their computing that surpasses description' (Basham, 1977, p. iv). Here, he is referring to the decimal place value system or the modern number system that we use today. Without this invention, modern civilisation would not have been possible.

Arab scholar Sa'id ibn Ahmad al-Andalusi (1029–1070) (1068, cited in Khan, 1991) declared that 'The first nation to have cultivated science is India. India is known for the wisdom of its people. Over many centuries, all kings of the past have recognised the ability of the Indians in all the branches of knowledge.'

François Voltaire (1694–1778), France's greatest writer and philosopher, enthused 'The *Veda* was the most precious gift for which the West had ever been indebted to the East.' He also stated 'I am convinced that everything has come down to us from the banks of the Ganges – astronomy, astrology, metempsychosis, etc.'

Lord Warren Hastings (1732–1818), the first governor-general of India, stated 'The writers of the Indian philosophies will survive, when the British dominion in India shall long have ceased to exist, and when the sources which it yielded of wealth and power are lost to remembrances.'

Jean Sylvain Bailly, great French astronomer and mathematician, noted for his computation of an orbit for Halley's Comet (1736–1793), concluded that 'The motion of the stars calculated by the Hindus before some 4,500 years vary not even a single minute from the modern tables of Cassin and Meyer that were used in Europe in the 19th century.'

Pierre-Simon Laplace (1749–1827), French astronomer and mathematician, maintained this:

> *It is India that gave us the ingenious method of expressing all numbers by means of ten symbols, each symbol receiving a value of position as well as an absolute value; a profound and important idea which appears so simple to us now that we ignore its true merit. But its very simplicity and the great ease which it has lent to computations put our arithmetic in the first rank of useful inventions; and we shall appreciate the grandeur of the achievement the more when we remember that it escaped the genius of Archimedes and Apollonius, two of the greatest men produced by antiquity.*

Mark Twain (1835–1910) – the celebrated American humourist, satirist, lecturer and writer – made many statements about India, including these:

- 'So far as I am able to judge, nothing has been left undone either by man or nature to make India the most extraordinary country that the sun visits on his rounds. Nothing seems to have been forgotten, nothing overlooked.'
- 'Land of religions, cradle of human race, birthplace of human speech, grandmother of legend, great grandmother of tradition. The land that all men desire to see and having seen once even by a glimpse, would not give that glimpse for the shows of the rest of the globe combined.'

- 'India had the start of the whole world in the beginning of things. She had the first civilization; she had the first accumulation of material wealth; she was populous with deep thinkers and subtle intellects; she had mines, and woods, and a fruitful soul.'

Lord Curzon (1859–1925), the viceroy of India from 1899 to 1905, expressed that 'India has left a deeper mark upon the history, philosophy and religion of mankind, than any other terrestrial unit in the universe.'

Will Durant (1885–1981), an American historian, stated this:

> *India was the motherland of our race and Sanskrit the mother of Europe's languages. India was the mother of our philosophy, of much of our mathematics, of the ideals embodied in Christianity, of self-government and democracy. In many ways Mother India is the Mother of us all.*

Romain Rolland (1866–1944), a French philosopher and Nobel laureate, asserted that 'If there is one place on the face of this Earth where all the dreams of living men have found a home from the very earliest days, when men began the dream of existence it is India.'

Albert Einstein (1879–1955) declared 'We owe a lot to the Indians, who taught us how to count, without which no worthwhile scientific discovery could have been possible.'

James Grant Duff (1759–1858) – a British soldier, historian of India and author of *A History of Marathas*, which is considered to be quite authoritative – proclaimed this:

> *Many of the advances in the sciences that we consider today to have been made in Europe were in fact made in India centuries ago. The place value system, the decimal system was developed in India in 100 BCE. Algebra, trigonometry and calculus came from India.*

Sir Isaac Newton (1643–1727) described how 'Hindus had an unbroken chain of natural wisdom which was as old as Abraham. The most ancient priests, the peaceful Brahmins possibly held the secrets of the world, both past and future' (Stuart, 2008).

Sir William Jones (1764–1794) – an Anglo-Welsh philologist, the greatest pioneer of orientalism in the 18th century and a scholar on ancient India – concluded 'Pythagoras and Plato derived their sublime theories from the sages of India' (Jones, 1807, p. 249). He also founded The Asiatic Society and delivered a lecture in 1786 in which he waxed lyrical about the Sanskrit language (Jones, 1807, p. 248):

> *The Sanskrit language, whatever be its antiquity, is of a wonderful structure; more perfect than the Greek, more copious than the Latin, and more exquisitely refined than either, yet bearing to both of them a stronger affinity, both in the roots of verbs and the forms of grammar, than could possibly have been produced by accident; so strong indeed, that no philologer could examine them all three, without believing them to have sprung from some common source, which, perhaps, no longer exists; there is a similar reason, though not quite so forcible, for supposing that both the Gothic and the Celtic, though blended with a very different idiom, had the same origin with the Sanskrit; and the old Persian might be added to the same family.*

Georg William Friedrich Hegel (1770–1831), one of the greatest German philosophers and writers, said 'It strikes everyone in beginning to form an acquaintance with the treasures of Indian literature, that a land so rich in intellectual products and those of the profoundest order of thought.'

Friedrich Von Schlegel (1772–1829) – a German writer, critic, philosopher, philologist and the most prominent founder of German Romanticism – asserted this:

> *There is no language in the world, even Greek, which has the clarity and the philosophical precision of Sanskrit. Great India is not only at the origin of everything, it is superior in everything, intellectually, religiously or politically and even the Greek heritage seems pale in comparison.*

Edgar Quinet (1803–1875), a French Historian, emphasised this:

> *When human revolutions first began, India stood more expressly than any other country for what may be called a 'Declaration of the Rights of the Being.' That divine Individuality, and its community with Infinity, is obviously the foundation and the source of all life and all history.* (Pragyata, 2018)

Henry David Thoreau (1817–1862) – the great American writer, philosopher, social critic and transcendentalist – confirmed the following:

> *Whenever I have read any part of the* Vedas, *I have felt that some unearthly and unknown light illuminated me. In the great teaching of the* Vedas, *there is no touch of sectarianism. It is of all ages, climbs and nationalities and is the royal road for the attainment of the great knowledge. When I read it, I feel that I am under the spangled heavens of a summer's night.*

Georg Morris Cohen Brandes (1842–1927) was born in Copenhagen of middle-class, Jewish parents. He was a Danish critic and scholar who had great influence on Scandinavian literature from the 1870s through to the turn of the 20th century. He said 'My spiritual home was on the banks of the Ganga [Ganges]' (Brandes, 1901).

William Butler Yeats (1856–1939) – the great Irish poet, dramatist, essayist and Nobel laureate – uttered 'It was my first meeting with Indian philosophy that confirmed my vague speculations and seemed at once logical and boundless.'

Ella Wheeler Wilcox (1850–1919), an American author and poet, maintained that '*Vedas* contain not only religious ideas for a perfect life, but also facts which science has proved true. Electricity, radium, electronics, airships, all were known to the seers of India.'

Niels Bohr (1885–1962) was a Danish nuclear physicist who developed the Bohr model of the atom, and who won the Nobel

Prize for Physics in 1922 for his theory of atomic structure. He stated, 'I go to the *Upanishads* to ask questions.'

Erwin Schrödinger (1887–1961), the Austrian-Irish physicist, famously declared:

> *Vedanta teaches that consciousness is singular, all happenings are played out in one universal consciousness and there is no multiplicity of selves... The stages of human development are to strive for Possession* (Artha), *Knowledge* (Dharma), *Ability* (Kama), *Being* (Moksha)... *Nirvana is a state of pure blissful knowledge. It has nothing to do with individuals. The ego or its separation is an illusion. The goal of man is to preserve his karma and to develop it further – when man dies his karma lives and creates for it another carrier.*

This quote clearly demonstrates Schrödinger's firm belief in reincarnation. He further said about the Indian influence 'Some blood transfusion from the East to the West is a must to save Western science from spiritual anaemia.'

Aldous Leonard Huxley (1894–1963) – a member of the famous, high-achieving Huxley family – was an English novelist, critic and philosopher, who was considered to be a pre-eminent intellectual of his time. He is the author of *Brave New World.* He pronounced 'Hinduism, the Perennial Philosophy that is at the core of all religions' (Huxley, 1945).

Nancy Wilson Ross (1901–1986) was an American who became an expert on Eastern religions; she was the author of several books including *The World of Zen* and *Time's Left Corner*. She wrote this (Wilson Ross, 1978, pp. 64–67):

> *Anachronistic as this labyrinthine mythology may appear to the foreign mind, many of India's ancient theories about the universe are startlingly modern in scope and worthy of a people who are credited with the invention of the zero, as well as algebra and its application of astronomy and geometry; a people who so carefully observed the heavens that, in the opinion of Monier-*

Williams, they determined the moon's synodical revolution much more correctly than the Greeks.

Many hundreds of years before those great European pioneers Galileo and Copernicus had to pay the heavy price of ridicule and excommunication for their daring theories, a section of the *Vedas*, known as the 'Brahmanas' was created, which contains this astounding statement:

> *The sun never sets or rises. When people think the sun is setting, he only changes about after reaching the end of the day and makes night below and day to what is on the other side. Then, when people think he rises in the morning, he only shifts himself about after reaching the end of the day night, and makes day below and night to what is on the other side. In truth, he does not see at all.*

Robert Oppenheimer (1904–1967), the American theoretical physicist known as 'the father of the atomic bomb', declared 'Access to the *Vedas* is the greatest privilege of this century.'

Fritjof Capra (born in 1939) – an Austrian-born American, eminent physicist and systems theorist – described the following (Capra, 1975):

> *To the Indian Rishis the divine play was the evolution of the cosmos through countless aeons. They say there are an infinite number of creations in an infinite universe. The Rishis gave the name* 'kalpa' *to the unimaginable span of time between the beginning and the end of creation. The time span is in millions of* kalpas. *One* kalpa *is about 4,320,000 years!*

Dr Carl Edward Sagan (1934–1996) – the American astronomer, cosmologist, astrophysicist and astrobiologist – believed that 'Hinduism is one of the only world's greatest faiths dedicated to the idea that the cosmos itself undergoes an immense, indeed an infinite number of deaths and rebirths. It is the only religion in which the time scales correspond to those of modern scientific cosmology.'

Georges Ifrah (born 1947), the French–Moroccan scholar and historian of mathematics – writes in his three-volume work *The Universal History of Numbers* (Ifrah, 1977):

> *Finally it has come to pass as though across the ages and civilizations, the human mind had tried all possible solutions to the problem of writing numbers, before universally adopting the one which seemed the most abstract, the most perfected and the most effective of all... The measure of genius of the Indian civilization, to which we owe our modern system, is all the greater in that it was the only one in all history to have achieved this triumph.*

Sir Charles Norton Edgcumbe Eliot (1862–1931), a British diplomat and colonial administrator, says (1921, cited in Anonymous, 1991, p. 369):

> *In Eastern Asia the influence of India has been notable in extent, strength, and duration. Scant justice is done to India's position in the world by those European histories which recount the exploits of her invaders and leave the impression that her own people were a feeble dreamy folk, surrendered from the rest of mankind by their seas and mountain frontiers. Such a picture takes no account of the intellectual conquests of the Hindus. Even their political conquests were not contemptible, and are remarkable for the distance, if not the extent, of the territories occupied... But such military or commercial invasions are insignificant compared with the spread of Indian thought. The south-eastern region of Asia – both mainland and archipelago – owed its civilization almost entirely to India. In Ceylon, Burma, Siam, Cambodia, Champa, and Java, religion, art, the alphabet, literature, as well as whatever science and political organization existed, were the direct gift of Hindus, whether Brahmin or Buddhists, and much the same may be said of Tibet, whence the wilder Mongols took as much Indian civilization as they could stomach.*

French scholar, Sylvain Levi (1863–1935) – an orientalist who wrote on Eastern religion, literature and history – was appointed as a lecturer at the school of higher studies in Paris (1886), taught Sanskrit at the Sorbonne (1889–1894) and wrote a doctoral dissertation called '*Le Théâtre Indien*' ('The Indian Theatre'). In *L'Inde et le Monde* (*India and the World*) (Nehru, 1990, pp. 200–210), he discussed India's role among nations:

> *From Persia to the Chinese Sea, from the icy regions of Siberia to the islands of Java and Borneo, from Oceania to Socotra, India has propagated her beliefs, her tales and her civilization. She has left indelible imprints on one-fourth of the human race in the course of a long succession of centuries. She has the right to reclaim in universal history the rank that ignorance has refused her for a long time and to hold her place amongst the great nations summarizing and symbolizing the spirit of Humanity.*

Sir Marc Aurel Stein (1862–1943), a Hungarian-born British archaeologist wrote this:

> *The vast extent of Indian cultural influences, from Central Asia in the North to tropical Indonesia in the South, and from the Borderlands of Persia to China and Japan, has shown that ancient India was a radiating centre of a civilization, which by its religious thought, its art and literature, was destined to leave its deep mark on the races wholly diverse and scattered over the greater part of Asia.*

According to A. L. Basham (1914–1986) – historian, Indologist and author (Basham, 1977, p. 485):

> *The whole of South-East Asia received most of its culture from India. In the 5th BC century colonists from Western India settled in* what is now Sri Lanka. *The Indian 'colonies' were peaceful ones, and the Indianized chieftains had learnt what India had to teach them.*

Sir John Marshall (1876–1958), the director general of the Archaeological Survey of India from 1902 to 1928 wrote this (Kainikara, 2016):

> *To know Indian art in India alone is to know but half its story. To apprehend it to the full, we must follow it to central Asia, China and Japan; we must watch it assuming new forms and breaking into new beauties as it spreads over Tibet and Burma and Siam; we must gaze in awe at the unexampled grandeur of its creations in Cambodia and Java. In each of these countries, Indian art encounters a different racial genius, a different local environment and under their modifying influence it takes on a different role.*

Conclusion

India, the ancient and living civilisation, continues its journey. Having started with nothing in 1947, India is today one of the world's biggest economies and is the largest democracy in the world.

India's spiritual values, its culture, and its aesthetic practices such as yoga are becoming increasingly popular all over the world. The Indian global diaspora is successful in terms of entrepreneurship as well as in the fields of medicine, science and technology. They have brought to their host countries India's spiritual and cultural values.

Over the decades and centuries to come, this ancient civilisation is destined to play a massive role at a global level.

Email : animalahimsa@gmail.com

Website : www.nitinmehta.co.uk

Nitin Mehta

01.01.2023

References

Acharya, A. (2021). 'Journey to the West': The Buddhist reimagination of China. *The Diplomat*. [online] Available at: https://thediplomat.com/2021/01/journey-to-the-west-the-buddhist-reimagination-of-china/

Aiyar, P. (2018). The Indian who docked in Osaka. *The Hindu*. [online] Available at: https://pallaviaiyar.com/2018/06/10/the-indian-who-docked-in-osaka/

Anonymous (1991). *Eminent Orientalists: Indian, European, American*. New Delhi: Asian Educational Services.

Aria Nuova (n.d.). *India and the Americas*. [online] Available at: https://www.arianuova.org/en/india-and-the-americas

Bartholomew, B Y (2017). Our unconscious soul: A re-look at Aristotle, Descartes & the *Upanishads*. *Universal Journal of Psychology*, *5*(6), pp. 272–282, DOI: 10.13189/ujp.2017.050605.

Basham, A L (1977). *The wonder that was India*. Reprint 2004. London: Picador.

Bayley, S (2004). Imagining 'Greater India': French and Indian visions of colonialism in the Indic mode. *Modern Asian Studies*, *38*(3), pp. 703–744, DOI: https://doi.org/10.1017/S0026749X04001246

Blair, E H and Robertson, J.A. (Eds.) (2004). *The Philippine islands 1493–1898, Vol. 4 of 55 1576–1582*. Project Gutenberg. Available at: gu012635.pdf (livrosgratis.com.br)

Brandes, G (1901). *Main currents in nineteenth century literature.* Reprint 2001. New York, NY: Adegi Graphics.

Brugsch, H K (1879). *A history of Egypt under the pharaohs, derived entirely from the monuments.* Translated by H.D. Seymour and edited and translated by P. Smith, 2015. Cambridge: Cambridge University Press.

Capra, F (1975). *The tao of physics.* Boulder, CO: Shambhala Publications.

Chulev, B (2016). *From Sanskrit to Macedonskrit.* [online] Available at: https://issuu.com/makedonskaakropola/docs/from_sanskrit_to_macedonskrit

Churchill, M H (1977). *Indian penetration of pre-Spanish Philippines: A new look at the evidence.* 15. Asian Center, University of the Philippines Diliman, pp. 21–45. [PDF] Available at: https://www.asj.upd.edu.ph/mediabox/archive/ASJ-15-1977/francisco-indian-prespanish-philippines.pdf

Cogniarchae (2016). *On some connections between ancient Slavs and India.* [online] Available at: https://cogniarchae.com/2016/02/05/on-some-connections-between-ancient-slavs-and-india/

Cogniarchae (2019). *Tracing the possible Slavic roots in Rigvedic India.* [online] https://cogniarchae.com/2019/07/30/slavic-roots-in-rigvedic-india/

Cooper, J (2015). Sanskrit in Croatia: From Sarasvati to Hrvati. *Sutra Journal.* [online] Available at: http://www.sutrajournal.com/sanskrit-in-croatia-from-sarasvati-to-hrvati-by-james-cooper

Das, V (2015). Shiva Linga in Ireland. IndiaDivine.org. [online] Available at: https://www.indiadivine.org/ancient-shiva-linga-in-ireland/

Deepak, B R (2020). Sanskrit had an influence on Chinese language. *Sunday Guardian Live.* [online] Available at: https://www.sundayguardianlive.com/opinion/sanskrit-influence-chinese-language

Dore, B (2015). In the world's largest Muslim nation, Hindu epics survive and thrive. *Quartz India*. [online] Available at: https://qz.com/india/456563/in-the-worlds-largest-muslim-nation-hindu-epics-survive-and-thrive/

Doshi, S (1993). *India and Egypt: Influences and interactions*. Hong Kong: South Asia Books.

Eliot, C N E (1921). *Hinduism and Buddhism: An historical sketch, volume 2*. Reprint 2019. Chennai: MJP Publishers.

Francisco, J (1994). *From Ayodhya to Pulu Agama Niog: Rama's journey to the Philippines*. Diliman: Asian Center, University of the Philippines.

Gallop, A T (2014). The *Ramayana* in Southeast Asia: (4) Indonesia and Malaysia. *British Library Asian and African studies blog*. [online] Available at: https://blogs.bl.uk/asian-and-african/2014/05/the-ramayana-in-southeast-asia-4-indonesia-and-malaysia.html?_ga=2.10128309.104194385.1617895758-217910864.1617895758

Ghosh, A and Kiparsky, P. (2019). The grammar of the elements. *American Scientist*, *107*(6), p. 350. DOI: 10.1511/2019.107.6.350

Hebner, J and Rosen, S (n.d.). The Heliodorus column. *Archaeology Online*. [online] Available at: https://www.archaeologyonline.net/artifacts/heliodorus-column

Heeren, A H L (1833). *Historical researches into the politics, intercourse, and trade of the principal nations of antiquity*. London: D.A. Tallboys.

Huxley, A L (1945). *The perennial philosophy*. Reprint 2009. New York, NY: Harper Perennial.

Ifrah, G (1977). *The universal history of numbers*. Reprint 2000. Hoboken, NJ: John Wiley & Sons.

Indian Diplomacy (2015). *Indian deities worshipped in Japan*. [video online] Available at: https://www.youtube.com/watch?v=8WaenzbSJwk&t=11s

Ishak, N (2019). Meet King Jayabaya, the Nostradamus of 12th-century Indonesia. *All That's Interesting*. [online] Available at: https://allthatsinteresting.com/jayabaya

Jones, W (1807). *Works volume 2*. London: J. Stockdale. [online] Available at: https://books.google.co.uk/books/about/Works.html?id=MNf3bgIGvpIC&redir_esc=y

Jones, W (1884). *Asiatic researches volume 1*. Calcutta: Brojendro Lall Doss. [online] Available at: https://archive.org/details/in.ernet.dli.2015.83879

Kainikara, S (2016). F*rom Indus to independence – A trek through Indian history: Vol II the classical age (adapted edition)*. New Delhi: VIJ Books (India) Pty Ltd.

Khan, M S (1991). Qādī Ṣā'id Al-Andalusī's Ṭabaqāt Al-Umam: The first world history of science. *Islamic Studies, 30*(4), pp. 517–540. [online] Available at http://www.jstor.org/stable/20840056

Khyentse Foundation (2015). *Part XI: King Jigme Dorje Wangchuck of Bhutan* (Patron King Series). [online] Available at: https://khyentsefoundation.org/project/576/

Knapp, S (2009). *Proof of Vedic culture's global existence*. Charleston, SC: BookSurge Publishing.

Knapp, S (2018). *History of Vedic culture in the Middle East*. [online] Available at: https://www.sanskritimagazine.com/history/history-of-vedic-culture-in-the-middle-east/

Lal, C (1940). *Hindu America*. Reprint 2016. New Delhi: Facsimile Publisher.

Lal, C (ed.) (1968). *India: The mother of us all*. Reprint 2013. New Delhi: Akshaya Prakashan.

Leider, J P (2006). Specialists for ritual, magic, and devotion: The court Brahmins (Punna) of the Konbaung kings (1752–1885). *The Journal of Burma Studies, 10*(2005/06), pp. 159–202. DOI: 10.1353/jbs.2005.0004

Londhe, S (2008). *A tribute to Hinduism: Thoughts and wisdom spanning continents and time about India and her culture.* New Delhi: Pragun Publication.

Lonely Tours (n.d.). *Royal Ballet Theatre.* [online] Available at: https://www.luangprabang-laos.com/Royal-Ballet-Theatre

Lopez, V F (1871). *Les races aryennes du Pérou: leur langue—leur religion—leur histoire.* Paris: L'Auteur. [online] Available at: https://archive.org/details/lesracesaryenne00lpgoog

Mandhani, N. (2018). The Indian princess who became a South Korean queen. *BBC News Delhi.* [online] Available at: https://www.bbc.co.uk/news/world-asia-india-46055285

McDaniel, J (2017). Religious change and experimentation in Indonesian Hinduism. *International Journal of Dharma Studies, 5*(20). DOI: https://doi.org/10.1186/s40613-017-0056-x

Mehta, N (2020). A nation born out of Sanskrit, and still in love with it. *Daily Guardian.* [online] Available at: https://thedailyguardian.com/a-nation-born-out-of-sanskrit-and-still-in-love-with-it/

Mena, R (1924). *Synthesis of Mexican archaeology for the summer school of the National University.* Translated from Spanish by John A. Jenkins. Mexico: Secretaria de Educacion Publica.

Merlin, M (2020). The Celtic-Vedic connection. *Sanskriti Magazine.* [online] Available at: https://www.sanskritimagazine.com/indian-religions/hinduism/the-celtic-vedic-connection/

Mishra, P (2020). The legends of *Mahabharata* and *Iliad. The Connectere.* [online] Available at: https://theconnectere.com/author/pallavi/page/2/

Nakamura, H (1992). Hinduism influence on Japanese culture. *Japan Times.* [online] Available at: https://www.sangam.org/2012/04/Hinduism_Japan.php

Nayyar, S (2017). India contribution to China. *eSamskriti.* [online] Available at: https://www.esamskriti.com/e/History/Indian-Influence-Abroad/India-contribution-to-China-1.aspx

Nehru, J (1990). *Discovery of India*. New Delhi: OUP India.

Neos Alexandria (n.d.). *Greco-Buddhism: A brief history*. [online] Available at: https://neosalexandria.org/syncretism/greco-buddhism-a-brief-history/

Office of International Religious Freedom (2021a). *2021 Report on International Religious Freedom: Bhutan*. US Department of State. [online] Available at: https://www.state.gov/reports/2021-report-on-international-religious-freedom/bhutan/

Office of International Religious Freedom (2021b). *2021 Report on International Religious Freedom: Mongolia*. US Department of State. [online] Available at: https://www.state.gov/reports/2021-report-on-international-religious-freedom/mongolia/

Open University, The (n.d.). *Making Britain: Purohit Swami*. [online] Available at: https://www.open.ac.uk/researchprojects/makingbritain/content/purohit-swami

Parker, B (2015). The forgotten Hindus of Vietnam's Champa Kingdom. *India Facts*. [online] Available at: http://indiafacts.org/forgotten-hindus-vietnams-champa-kingdom/

Pocoke, E (1852). *India in Greece*. Reprint 2015. New Delhi: Rupa Publications.

Poindexter, M (1930). *The Ayar-Incas*. Volumes 1 and 2. New York, NY: Horace Liveright.

Polish History Museum (n.d.). The passage to India. *Google Arts & Culture*. [online] Available at: https://artsandculture.google.com/exhibit/passage-to-india-polish-history-museum/FQKCQq9LDKemIg?hl=en

Pragyata (2018). *15 June*. [online] Available at: https://twitter.com/Pragyata_/status/1007516307288281088

Preston, D. (2015). Exclusive: Lost city discovered in the Honduran Rain Forest. *National Geographic*. [online] Available at: https://www.nationalgeographic.com/adventure/article/150302-honduras-lost-city-monkey-god-maya-ancient-archaeology

Rawson, P S (1967). *The art of Southeast Asia*. London: Thames and Hudson Ltd.

'Reamker' (2021). *Wikipedia*. [online] Available at: https://en.wikipedia.org/wiki/Reamker (Accessed 9 April 2021).

Roberts, P W (2007). *Empire of the soul*. New Delhi: Matrix Digital Publishing.

Royal Historical Commission of Burma (1829–1832). *Hmannan Yazawin* (in Burmese). 1–3 (2003 ed.). Yangon: Ministry of Information, Myanmar.

Royal Thai Embassy (2018). *'The Kings and I(ndia)': The royal Thai family and the Siam-Bharat relations*. [online] Available at: http://newdelhi.thaiembassy.org/en/2018/07/kings-india-royal-thai-family-context-siam-bharat-relations/

Serkeen (2017). Ancient Celtic Druids and the *Bhagavad Gita. Red Branch Chronicles*. [online] Available at: https://celticcurve.com/2017/03/13/ancient-celtic-druids-and-the-bhagavad-gita/

Simha, R K (2014). *Sanskrit and Russian: Ancient kinship*. [online] Available at: https://www.rbth.com/blogs/2014/11/01/sanskrit_and_russian_ancient_kinship_39451#:~:text=Colonial%20era%20linguist%20William%20Jones,more%20exquisitely%20refined%20than%20either.%E2%80%9D&text=Vedic%20Sanskrit%20-was%20spoken%20as,of%20years%20from%20that%20date.

Stuart, T (2008). *The bloodless revolution: A cultural history of vegetarianism from 1600 to modern times*. New York, NY: W. W. Norton & Company.

Sukarno, S (1946). [Special article – title unknown]. *The Hindu*, 4 January.

Swami, I (1996). *Chapter-22: The Russian Veda*. [online] Available at: https://www.indradyumnaswami.com/writings/books/diary/volume-2/chapter-22-russian-veda/

Universal Theosophy (2020). *Plato's chariot allegory, with the commentary of Hermeas.* [online] Available at: https://universaltheosophy.com/articles/platos-chariot-allegory-with-the-commentary-of-hermeas/

Vedavyas, E (1995). *Hinduism in the space age.* Hyderabad: United Social Cultural & Educational Foundation of India.

Wilson Ross, N (1978). *Three ways of Asian wisdom: Hinduism, Buddhism, Zen and their significance for the West.* New York, NY: Simon & Schuster.

Woźnica, P (2010). Remarks on Sanskrit and Pali loanwords in Khmer. *Investigationes Linguisticae, XX* (2010).

'Ynglism' (2021). (2021). *Wikipedia.* [online] Available at: https://en.wikipedia.org/wiki/Ynglism (Accessed 8 June 2021).

Photograph References

Adityamadhav83 (2010). *Lord Narasimha statue on walls of Simhachalam Temple*. [online] Available at: https://commons.wikimedia.org/wiki/File:Lord_Narasimha_statue_on_walls_of_Simhachalam_Temple.jpg. CC BY-SA 3.0.

Chez Cåsver (Xuan Che) (2008). *A Buddhist stupa in the collection of the Palace Museum, Beijing*. [online] Available at: https://commons.wikimedia.org/w/index.php?curid=15117110. CC BY-SA 2.0.

Cmichel67 (2016). *Prambanan Temple Yogyakarta Indonesia*. [online] Available at: https://commons.wikimedia.org/w/index.php?curid=47964480. CC BY-SA 4.0.

Dilipkumarftii1977 (2020). *Heliodorus pillar (cropped)*. [online] Available at: https://commons.wikimedia.org/w/index.php?curid=85718174. CC BY-SA 4.0.

DoktorMax (2007). *Tra Kieu Pedestal*. [online] Available at: https://commons.wikimedia.org/w/index.php?curid=4262476. Public domain.

Eichmann, G (1980). *Copán in Honduras*. [online] Available at: https://commons.wikimedia.org/wiki/File:Copan-46-Hanuman-1980-gje.jpg. CC BY-SA 4.0.

Fabio from Rome, Italy (2008). *Benzaiten*. [online] Available at: https://commons.wikimedia.org/w/index.php?curid=6445084. CC BY-SA 2.0.

Grueslayer (2016). *Hanuman statue, Carapichaima, Couva-Tabaquite-Talparo, Trinidad and Tobago*. [online] Available at: https://

commons.wikimedia.org/w/index.php?curid=54541297. CC BY-SA 4.0.

HiraV (2016). *Makindu Gurdwara*. [online] Available at: https://commons.wikimedia.org/w/index.php?curid=48583274. CC BY-SA 4.0.

Hollmann, D (2013). *The lion man from the Stadel cave in the Hohlenstein, Lonetal (Bade-Wurtemberg).* [online] Available at: https://commons.wikimedia.org/w/index.php?curid=29686577. CC BY-SA 4.0.

Hybernator (2007). *Statute of Vishnu at the Nat-Hlaung Kyaung Temple, Pagan (Bagan).* [online] Available at: https://commons.wikimedia.org/w/index.php?curid=18158532. CC BY-SA 3.0.

JohnJDuncan (2012). *Lia Fail.* [online] Available at: https://commons.wikimedia.org/wiki/File:Lia_Fail.jpg. CC BY-SA 4.0.

Jpatokal (n.d.). *Scene from the* Ramakien (Thai Ramayana) *depicted on a mural at Wat Phra Kaew (Temple of the Emerald Buddha), Bangkok, Thailand.* [online] Available at: https://commons.wikimedia.org/w/index.php?curid=6625422. Public domain.

Мариньо, В (1995). *Mastelninsa in Moscow 1995.* Mos.ru. [online] Available at: https://commons.wikimedia.org/wiki/File:Lia_Fail.jpg. CC BY-SA 4.0.

Public.Resource.Org (2017). *Pompeii Indian statuette front and back.* [online] Available at: https://commons.wikimedia.org/w/index.php?curid=61992663. Public domain.

Reitveld, A (1975). *Jains Hindu temple, Mombasa.* [online] Available at: https://commons.wikimedia.org/w/index.php?curid=82767685. CC BY-SA 4.0.

Rémi Cormier (2007). *Tomb of King Suro's queen: Heo Hwang-ok.* [online] Available at: https://commons.wikimedia.org/wiki/File:Queen_Suro_Tomb.jpg. CC BY-SA 3.0.

Sailko (2013). *Secret Cabinet in the Museo Archeologico (Naples).* [online] Available at: https://commons.wikimedia.org/

wiki/File:Statuetta_indiana_di_Lakshmi,_avorio,_da_pompei,_1-50_dc_ca.,_149425,_02.JPG. CC BY-SA 3.0.

Sailko (2016). *Collections of the Field Museum of Natural History.* [online] Available at: https://commons.wikimedia.org/w/index.php?curid=65575658. CC BY-SA 3.0.

Sebastian, M (2009). *Statue in Ta Reach, Cambodia.* [online] Available at: https://commons.wikimedia.org/w/index.php?curid=20044610. CC BY-SA 2.0.

Unknown (n.d.). Reproduced with due thanks to the copyright holder, who could not be located despite the reasonable efforts of the author.

WikiLaurent (2010). *Panorama of Boddhisatvas in the main Longmen Grotto.* [online] Available at: https://commons.wikimedia.org/w/index.php?curid=12100816. CC BY-SA 3.0.